Christ's Call
TO REFORM
the Church

TIMELESS DEMANDS
FROM THE LORD TO HIS PEOPLE

JOHN
MacARTHUR

MOODY PUBLISHERS

CHICAGO

All Scripture quotations, unless otherwise indicated, are taken from the New American Standard Bible®, Copyright © 1960, 1962, 1963, 1968, 1971, 1972, 1973, 1975, 1977, 1995 by The Lockman Foundation. Used by permission. (www.Lockman.org)
Scripture quotations marked KJV are taken from the King James Version.

Edited by Kevin P. Emmert
Interior and cover design: Erik M. Peterson
Cover and interior dingbats copyright © 2014 by Yulia_Malinovskaya/iStock. All rights reserved.

All websites listed herein are accurate at the time of publication but may change in the future or cease to exist. The listing of website references and resources does not imply publisher endorsement of the site's entire contents. Groups and organizations are listed for informational purposes, and listing does not imply publisher endorsement of their activities.

Library of Congress Cataloging-in-Publication Data

Names: MacArthur, John, 1939- author.
Title: Christ's call to reform the church : timeless demands from the Lord to his people / John MacArthur.
Description: Chicago : Moody Publishers, 2018. | Includes bibliographical references.
Identifiers: LCCN 2018026071 (print) | LCCN 2018034393 (ebook) | ISBN 9780802495600 (ebook) | ISBN 9780802415707 | ISBN 9781593286729 (BGEA Edition)
Subjects: LCSH: Bible. Revelation, I-III--Criticism, interpretation, etc. | Church renewal--Biblical teaching.
Classification: LCC BS2825.6.C5 (ebook) | LCC BS2825.6.C5 M33 2018 (print) | DDC 228/.06--dc23
LC record available at https://lccn.loc.gov/2018026071

ISBN: 978-0-8024-1570-7

We hope you enjoy this book from Moody Publishers. Our goal is to provide high-quality, thought-provoking books and products that connect truth to your real needs and challenges. For more information on other books and products written and produced from a biblical perspective, go to www.moodypublishers.com or write to:

Moody Publishers
820 N. LaSalle Boulevard
Chicago, IL 60610

1 3 5 7 9 10 8 6 4 2

Printed in the United States of America

To Bob and Linda McIntyre—dear, devoted friends and precious partners in ministry. Your sacrificial service for the cause of Christ is a powerful encouragement and a vibrant example to me, and to all of us in the Grace to You family.

Contents

Introduction

In the book of Revelation, Jesus wrote seven letters to cities in Asia Minor. He didn't write them to city hall; He wrote them to the church.

Let that sink in for a moment. In the closing chapters of Scripture, the Lord did not set His church on a mission to "redeem the culture." He didn't advise His people to leverage political power to institute morality, or to protest the rule of immoral men. In fact, He didn't launch a social revolution or devise a political strategy of any kind.

The church today—and particularly the church in America—needs to understand that God has not called His people out of the world simply to wage a culture war with the world. We're not meant to gain temporal ground, like some invading force working to superficially "turn this country back to God." We need to shed the illusion that our ancestors' morality once made America a "Christian nation." There have never been any Christian nations—just Christians.

Believers need to understand that what happens in America politically and socially has nothing to do with the progress or the power of the kingdom of God. Cultural change can't accelerate the kingdom's growth; nor can it hinder it (see Matt. 16:18). Christ's kingdom "is not of this world" (John 18:36).

That's not to say I'm dismissive of our democratic process or ungrateful to have a voice in it. It's a great blessing to have a vote and to be able to support biblical standards of morality. Many Christians throughout the history of the church have lived through far worse circumstances than ours, with no legal means to do anything about it.

But the presumption that a social movement or political clout could make a significant spiritual difference in the world is evidence of a severe misunderstanding of sin. Believers need to put our energies into ministry that can transform lives, not into laws. The work of God's kingdom is not about overhauling governments, rewriting regulations, or rebuilding society into some version of a Christian utopia. Political and social justice efforts are, at best, short-term, external solutions for society's moral ills, and they do *nothing* to address the personal, internal, dominant matter of sinful hearts that hate God (see Rom. 8:7), and can be rescued from eternal death only by faith in the Lord Jesus Christ.

MORALITY DAMNS

Morality on its own is no solution; it damns just like immorality. Morality cannot turn the stony heart to flesh, it cannot break the chains of sin, and it cannot reconcile us to God. In that sense, morality alone is as empty to save as any satanic religion.

Jesus went head to head with the most religious and outwardly moral people in His world, particularly with the priests, scribes, and experts in Old Testament law. He said, "I did not come to call the righteous, but sinners" (Mark 2:17). And in Matthew 23, He unleashed His most searing accusations against the religious right of His day, the party of the Pharisees. These were the most pious men in the nation, who fastidiously kept of the law of God and faithfully followed rabbinical tradition. Jesus says, "Woe to you, scribes and Pharisees, hypocrites" (v. 13). The word "woe" is the equivalent of saying "curse you." He's pronouncing damnation and judgment on them. He repeats the same phrase over and over in the subsequent verses. He calls them "blind guides" in verse 16, as they led Israel astray through their empty, pious morality.

Neither social change nor moralism were ever the message of the Old Testament prophets. They were never the message of the Messiah or the New Testament writers. Such has never been God's message to the world at all. In fact, Isaiah tells us that "all our righteous deeds are like a filthy garment" (Isa. 64:6). Man's morality at its apex is nothing more than foul, defiled rags.

Moreover, Romans says, "There is none righteous . . . there is none who does good, there is not even one" (3:10–12). So whatever imaginary righteousness man has, whatever superficial morality he exhibits, is just a charade. There is no one righteous, no matter what kind of pious façade people put up.

People *can* change their lives. They can have a moment of crisis and decide they're going to turn away from immorality or addiction and start living a better life. People can, to some degree, clean up their act simply by applying extraordinary human effort and resolve. If enough of them do it, there can be a slight moral upgrade in human society. But behavioral reform has no bearing on people's relationship with God. It has no means to deliver them out of the bondage of sin into the kingdom of Christ. The best that morality can do is turn people into another batch of condemned Pharisees. Morality can't save anyone from guilt or fuel genuine godliness. Pharisees and prostitutes share the same hell.

The push for cultural morality or even social justice is a dangerous distraction from the work of the church. It wastes immense amounts of precious resources, including time, money, and energy. Ephesians 5:16–17 urges believers to "[make] the most of your time, because the days are evil. So then do not be foolish, but understand what the will of the Lord is." And the will of the Lord is not a culture governed by social equity or even institutionalized Phariseeism.

The word *evangelical* is derived from the Greek word for "gospel." It originally signified Christians who understood that the gospel is the core and the very essence of Christian doctrine and therefore must be guarded at all costs. But it has been so painted over with social and political colors as to have become a political term, rejected by most of society and even most professing Christians.

THE TRUE CALLING OF THE CHURCH

The will of God is *not* that we become so politicized that we turn our mission field into our enemy. Christians are right to repudiate sin, and to declare without equivocation that sin is an offense to our holy God. That includes sins like abortion, homosexuality, sexual promiscuity, and any other sins that our corrupt culture says we must accept. But a culture sold out to sins such as those is not going to be turned around—much less won over—by angry protests and partisan politics. It's futile to think the solution to our culture's moral bankruptcy is a legislative remedy. There is no law that can make fallen sinners righteous (see Gal. 2:21).

Timothy ministered in a culture that was at least as bad as ours. Nothing in Paul's instructions to his younger disciple suggested that Timothy should try to redeem *the culture*. Indeed, he told Timothy things would get even worse (2 Tim. 3:13). What the people of this depraved world need is the gospel. They need to be told that their sins can be forgiven and they can be set free from the chains of sin and this world's system. Believers have no right to regard lost sinners with contempt or loathing. Our attitude toward our neighbors should be a reflection of Christ's love for them, not an expression of our disagreement with their politics or even their morality. We have no right to withhold the good news of salvation from them, like Jonah tried to do with the Ninevites. We ought to make sure that the lost sinners in our lives know that we love them enough to offer them God's forgiveness. There is a holy hatred for sin, but even Christ could weep over the lost in sympathy, and so must we.

The world is the way it is today because it is the world, and the church must confront it with the full truth. It's hypocritical for Christians to berate the secular world for the way unbelievers behave when so many churches are validating it either by believing in its ability to be redeemed by human power or by putting on a worldly circus of entertainment and cheap distractions from the real issues. It's time for the church to be about the ministry of reconciliation—for God's people to boldly and faithfully proclaim His gospel and for His church to be salt and light in this dark and desperate world (Matt. 5:13–16). That was the Lord's message to the churches in Revelation. He commanded them to put off worldliness and corruption, to renew their love for Him, and to guard the purity of His gospel and His church. Virtually every admonition, rebuke, warning, and call to repentance our Lord makes in these letters is applicable to the church in the twenty-first century—including many of today's best-known and most-influential evangelical churches. It's time for us to pay attention to the letters to those churches in Revelation and heed Christ's call to reform His church.

1

Calling the Church to Repent

Have you ever heard of a church that repented? Not individuals, but an entire church that collectively recognized its congregational transgressions and openly, genuinely repented, with biblical sorrow and brokenness?

Sadly, you probably have not.

For that matter, have you ever heard of a pastor who called his church to repent and threatened his congregation with divine judgment if they failed to do so?

It's not likely. Pastors today seem to have a hard enough time calling individuals to repent, let alone calling the whole church to account for their corporate sins. In fact, if a pastor were so bold as to lead his own church to repent, he might not be the pastor for much longer. At minimum, he would face resistance and scorn from within the congregation. That inevitable backlash is likely strong enough to generate a kind of preemptive fear, keeping most church leaders from ever considering a call for corporate repentance.

On the other hand, if a pastor or church leader has the temerity to call for *another* church—rather than his own—to repent, he will almost certainly be accused of being critical, divisive, and over-stepping his authority. He'll face a chorus of voices telling him to mind his own business. Vilifying him, therefore, clears a path for the confronted church to sidestep his admonition altogether.

The fact is churches rarely repent. Churches that start down a path of worldliness, disobedience, and apostasy typically move even further from orthodoxy over time. They almost never recover their original soundness. Rarely are they broken over their collective sins against the Lord. Rarely do they turn aside from corruption, immorality, and false doctrine. Rarely do they cry out from the depths of their hearts for forgiveness, cleansing, and restoration. Most never even consider it, because they have become comfortable with their condition.

In reality, calling the church to repent and reform can be very dangerous. Church history is replete with examples.

THE GREAT EJECTION

The name "Puritan" was devised as a term of derision and scorn. It was applied to a group of Anglican pastors in England in the sixteenth and seventeenth centuries who sought to purify the church of its remaining Roman Catholic influences and practices. These Puritan pastors repeatedly called for the churches of England to repent of their extensive carnality, heresy, and priestly corruption. But the Anglican Church would not repent. They could not deny the need for reformation, but they wanted a "middle way" rather than a thorough reformation.

Those who held the reins in the Anglican hierarchy remained impenitent—but not passive. They were determined to silence the voices calling them to repentance. For decades, the Puritans faced hostility and persecution from church leaders and political rulers alike. Many suffered and died for their faith, while many more endured imprisonment and torture for the sake of Christ. The persecution reached a crescendo in 1662, when the English Parliament issued the Act of Uniformity. The decree essentially outlawed anything other than strict Anglican doctrine and practice. That led to a monumental and tragic day in England's spiritual history: August 24, 1662, commonly known as the Great Ejection. On that day, two thousand Puritan pastors were stripped of their ordination and permanently thrown out of their Anglican churches.

Those faithful Puritans understood that the Church of England had to repent and reform before the nation would ever turn to Christ. But rather than reject their wickedness and corruption, the impenitent leaders of the Church of England attempted to silence anyone calling for repentance and restoration.

Subsequent history reveals that the Great Ejection was no isolated event with temporary significance. The spiritual turmoil did not end once the Puritans were excommunicated and separated from their congregations. In fact, it's safe to say that the Great Ejection was a spiritual disaster that serves as a clear and dark dividing line in England's history that has implications to the present day.

One of those ejected ministers was Matthew Meade. Concerning the Great Ejection, he wrote, "This fatal day deserves to be written in black letters in England's calendar."[1] Iain Murray describes the spiritual fallout of that dark day: "After the silencing of the 2,000, we enter an age of rationalism, of coldness in the pulpit and indifference in the pew, an age in which scepticism and worldliness went far to reducing national religion to a mere parody of New Testament Christianity."[2]

J. B. Marsden saw the event as an invitation for the Lord's judgment. He wrote, "If it be presumptuous to fix upon particular occurrences as proofs of God's displeasure; yet none will deny that a long, unbroken, course of disasters indicates but too surely, whether to a nation or a church, that his favour is withdrawn. Within five years of the ejection of the two thousand nonconformists, London was twice laid waste."[3] He wasn't wrong. The Great Ejection occurred in the summer of 1662. In 1665, an epidemic of the bubonic plague struck London, killing more than 100,000 people, roughly one quarter of its population. The following year, a massive fire swept through London, incinerating more than 13,000 homes, nearly a hundred churches—including St. Paul's Cathedral—and decimating most of the city. Many historians agreed with Marsden, viewing those disasters as divine retribution for England's impenitence.

Still, those disasters don't compare to the spiritual consequences of England's apostasy. After citing the plague and the fire, Marsden continued, "Other calamities ensued, more lasting and far more terrible. Religion in the church of England was almost extinguished, and in many of her parishes the lamp of God went out."[4]

J. C. Ryle, who served as the bishop of Durham in the late 1800s, summed up the spiritual cost of the Anglican Church's impenitence this way: "I believe [the Great Ejection] did an injury to the cause of true religion in England, which will probably never be repaired."[5] Indeed, over the centuries that followed, England has succumbed to a culture of liberalism, overrun with cold, dead churches and awash in apostasy and spiritual darkness.

And despite the centuries of foul fruit that sprang from the Act of Uniformity and the Great Ejection, the Church of England failed to achieve its primary goal. The Puritans were scattered, but not silenced. Many of the men who were ejected from their churches went on to have influence that continues to this day. Spiritual stalwarts such as Richard Baxter, John Flavel, Thomas Brooks, and Thomas Watson were among those who lost their pulpits in 1662 but faithfully carried on as outlaw preachers. Along with many others, they continued to expose the corruption of the Anglican Church, calling for its repentance. In that sense, they carried on the legacy that began with the Reformers more than a century earlier.

THE LEGACY OF THE REFORMATION

In medieval Europe, the Roman Catholic Church had a stranglehold on all matters pertaining to spiritual life. In an era when Bibles were rare and inaccessible to all but the clergy, the hierarchy of Rome established itself as the gatekeeper, controlling access to Scripture, and thus to God. The priests granted forgiveness, bestowed blessing, and served as the arbiters of eternal reward.

By the 1400s, the church was overrun with layers of institutional corruption. Behind a transparent veil of piety, immorality and wickedness permeated the church. Throughout Christendom, church parishioners struggled to survive and eke out a humble existence, while the religious ruling class preyed on the people's ignorance to line their pockets and expand their authority. Popes and archbishops lived reprobate lives of lavish excess and wanton lasciviousness. The church ruled with an iron fist, overseeing even governments and influencing all aspects of medieval life.

To its core, the medieval Roman Catholic Church was a breeding ground for heresy and spiritual deception. But even in the midst of its dominating corruption, the Lord was still redeeming His own and building His true church. Some churches existed and even thrived outside of Rome's authority. The Lord also used bold and faithful men like John Wycliffe and John Huss to reject and repudiate extrabiblical Catholic dogma, to peel back its pious mask and expose the corruption within. Like the Puritans centuries later in England, these men did not seek to overthrow the church, but hoped to call it to repentance and help restore it to biblical orthodoxy. And for their efforts, both men were excommunicated and burned as heretics. (Wycliffe was retroactively excommunicated decades after his death. His body was actually exhumed and incinerated, his bones crushed, and the bones and ashes scattered in the River Swift.)

Although the Catholic Church went to extreme measures to

silence Wycliffe, Huss, and others like them, the truth they preached survived and paved the way for an earnest German monk to carry on their legacy and strike a decisive blow against the papal fortress. Like those before him, Martin Luther did not set out on an overtly rebellious course to overthrow or upend the Church. But out of his fervent study of Scripture and through the illumination of the Holy Spirit, Luther came to a saving knowledge of the Lord Jesus Christ and to a clear understanding of Rome's deviation from the truth of the gospel.

Historians identify the flashpoint of the Reformation as October 31, 1517, the day Luther nailed his Ninety-Five Theses to the door of the Castle Church in Wittenberg. In that pivotal treatise, Luther, not yet converted, argued against the abusive traditions of the Catholic Church—particularly the sale of indulgences.

Indulgences were a means for Catholics to buy their way out of penance and purgatory. They could also be purchased on behalf of deceased loved ones. With an extremely high mortality rate and an equally short life expectancy—and with the church's threat of eons in purgatory constantly hanging overhead—most people would leap at any hope to avoid languishing in the afterlife, in some holding place short of heaven.

Under Pope Leo X, the medieval church used the sale of indulgences to support the construction of elaborate structures like St. Peter's Basilica in Rome.[6] A savvy monk named Johann Tetzel was one of their most successful salesmen.

Tetzel was ingenious in his mischief, perfecting a masterful sales pitch to prey on the credulous simplicity of Catholic parishioners. He would famously exhort the crowds with the promise, "As soon as the coin in the coffer rings, the soul from purgatory springs." To a customer base of illiterate, superstitious peasants, what greater hope could there be?

Luther was furious over Tetzel's church-sponsored extortion. His Ninety-Five Theses constituted a public repudiation of the practice and a direct assault on the greed of the Church. Thesis eighty-six put the blame squarely on Pope Leo himself: "Why does not the pope, whose wealth is today greater than the wealth of the richest Crassus, build this one basilica of St. Peter with his own money rather than with the money of poor believers?"

Those Ninety-Five Theses ignited the Reformation, but they did not constitute its primary battleground. In fact, Luther had not yet come to true faith and repentance at the time of their writing—he was saved shortly thereafter. The doctrine of justification by faith is of course an insurmountable argument against the sale of indulgences, so it is significant that the Ninety-Five Theses omit any mention of that doctrine. It indicates that Luther's "Tower Experience," when he finally understood what it means to be justified by faith alone, occurred sometime after the posting of the theses. Scholars and historians cannot determine the precise year when Luther first had his awakening, but Luther spoke of it often, and he seemed to view it as the moment of his true conversion. Here's how he described what happened:

> The words "righteous" and "righteousness of God" struck my conscience like lightning. When I heard them I was exceedingly terrified. If God is righteous [I thought], he must punish. But when by God's grace I pondered, in the tower and heated room of this building, over the words, "He who through faith is righteous shall live" [Romans 1:17] and "the righteousness of God" [Romans 3:21], I soon came to the conclusion that if we, as righteous men, ought to live from faith and if the righteousness of God contribute to the salvation of all who believe, then salvation won't be our merit but God's mercy. My spirit was thereby cheered. For it's by the righteousness of God that we're justified and saved through Christ. These words [which had before terrified me] now became more

pleasing to me. The Holy Spirit unveiled the Scriptures for me in this tower.[7]

The truth that believers are justified by faith alone became the focus of the entire reformation debate. That principle (*sola fide*) is therefore known as the *material principle* of the Reformation. But it was the *formal principle* of the Reformation, *sola Scriptura*—the authority and sufficiency of Scripture—that motivated Luther to write and post the Ninety-Five Theses. His commitment to that principle was evident even in his earliest writings before his conversion.

John Calvin, Ulrich Zwingli, Philip Melanchthon, Theodore Beza, John Knox, and many more shared that same conviction and fought the same fight on different fronts to rescue and preserve the authority of God's Word in His church against the tyranny of the pope and the heresies of the Catholic Church. The supremacy and authority of Scripture was the beating heart of the Reformation from which all its other core tenets flowed.

In defense of his work at the Diet of Worms, Luther famously proclaimed his submission to Scripture alone:

> Unless I am convinced by the testimony of the Scriptures or by clear reason (for I do not trust either in the pope or in councils alone, since it is well known that they have often erred and contradicted themselves), I am bound by the Scriptures I have quoted and my conscience is captive to the Word of God. I cannot and will not retract anything, since it is neither safe nor right to go against conscience. May God help me. Amen.[8]

Five hundred years later, faithful men serve in the shadow of these great warriors of God and work to carry on their legacy of biblical fidelity and gospel truth. Moreover, we carry on their protest, not merely against Rome, but against any system, church, or self-styled shepherd who deviates from the Word of God in the life of the church. And tragically, the twenty-first century church may be facing greater threats than it ever endured under Rome.

THE PATHOLOGY OF AN APOSTATE CHURCH

Consider the spiritual ground that is lost when the church surrenders biblical authority. If Scripture does not speak with absolute, inerrant authority, the offer of justification by grace through faith cannot be extended to desperate sinners. One can't argue for the sufficiency of Christ as the sacrifice for sins, or His rule as the Head of the church. One can't cling to the glorious truth of imputation—that at the cross, "[God] made Him who knew no sin to be sin on our behalf, so that we might become the righteousness of God in Him" (2 Cor. 5:21). Without those truths, we have no guarantee that God's wrath has been satisfied. There can be no assurance of faith, no hope of heaven, and no confidence in the promises of God.

On the other hand, doing away with the authority of Scripture—or merely subjugating it to the authority of men—purposely paves the way for false doctrine and false teachers to infiltrate the flock of God. It invites theological confusion, elevating the words of fallible men over the inerrant Word of God. It is designed to exchange the gospel of grace for a man-centered system of works-righteousness. And it pollutes the purity of God's truth, clouding biblical doctrine with superstition, tradition, extra-biblical revelation, and demonic deception.

That's a broad way to summarize the various deviations that have dominated the Roman Catholic Church since before the time of Luther. But it's also a fitting description of the Protestant church *today*. If that sounds like an overstatement, consider these questions: What demonstrable difference is there between Tetzel's indulgences and the holy water and anointed scraps of cloth peddled by charismatic charlatans to their vast audiences? What's the difference between a pope who speaks *ex cathedra* and a pastor who exposits his own dreams and mental impressions as fresh revelation from the Lord? And what separates the worship of Mary and the veneration of the saints from the way today's self-proclaimed apostles visit the graves of their forebears to "soak" in the deceased's anointing?

Worse still, the same kinds of rampant corruption and immorality the Roman Church once worked to conceal are now celebrated and encouraged by many Protestant congregations. Far from being known for their *purity*, many churches today go out of their way to embrace or imitate the debauchery of secular culture. Pastors exegete Hollywood movies rather than Scripture. Seeker-sensitive megachurch gatherings often look and feel more like a rock concert or a burlesque show than a worship service. Celebrity-minded church leaders seem more interested in what's stylish and marketable than they are in what's sound and solidly biblical. Shockingly, there are even some ostensibly evangelical churches whose leaders are proud that their membership is open, welcoming, über-tolerant, or even affirming toward serial adulterers, hard-hearted fornicators, impenitent homosexuals, immoral idol worshipers, and even to forms of paganism. They're *proud* of it.

Many more congregations are on a slower path to the same destination. While they might not openly celebrate immorality, they do nothing to drive it from their midst. Sin is not confronted and church discipline is not faithfully practiced. Over time, the conscience—both individually and collectively—grows cold, unconfessed sin becomes the norm, and the church bears no discernable difference from the world.

All that is evidence of a lack of submission to God's Word and a decreasing concern for doctrinal truth and the purity and protection it produces. Born from the conviction that true believers must separate from an apostate church, Protestantism has needed only a scant five hundred years to cultivate its own strains of apostasy. Much like the Israelites in the book of Judges, the Protestant church seems determined to repeat the mistakes of its past rather than learn from them. Paul's indictment of the churches of Galatia applies to much of the evangelical church: "You foolish Galatians, who has bewitched you, before whose eyes Jesus Christ was publicly portrayed as crucified?" (Gal 3:1). A recent national survey revealed that 52 percent of evangelical Protestants believe salvation comes by faith and works combined. Only 30 percent affirm *sola fide* and *sola Scriptura*.[9] The Reformation is being undone by "bewitched" evangelical Protestants. The protest is largely over.

Descent into apostasy doesn't happen overnight; the changes are slow and steady. Rejecting Scripture's authority and priority is the first step, usually followed by a succession of compromises: *maybe we can be more relevant and inviting to the world if we don't take this verse or that sin too seriously*. Once the church determines its purpose is to engage and attract the culture rather than edify and equip the saints, it sets out on a path that will always lead to worldliness and apostasy. Not long ago, the pastor of one of the largest churches in America told church leaders they should not let doctrine get in the way of winning people over. One sympathetic author summed up his exhortation succinctly: "Don't put theology above ministry."[10] Churches today are so invested in attracting sinners that they attempt to bury their theology under the welcome mat.

That unbiblical model of outreach is the very thing dulling many churches' ability to reach the world with the gospel. Filling the pews with comfortable, unaffected unbelievers is the fastest way to confuse and corrupt the work of the church. God has not called His people out of the world to chase its trends in vain attempts to seem relevant. The church cannot be salt and light in this wretched world if we are indistinguishable from worldly people (see Matt. 5:13–16).

THE ALLEGED ADVANTAGES OF THE EARLY CHURCH

To curb those worldly trends and simplify the work of ministry, some Christians today are calling for a return to the early church model. They believe what's ailing and inhibiting the work of the church today is the church structure itself. Megachurches with sprawling campuses, legions of leaders, and overgrown congregations that must be endlessly subdivided—those are supposedly the villains that have corrupted and confused the church in recent years.

The argument suggests that Christians can't function and serve to their full potential in a large-church environment, and that the New Testament model of small house churches frees God's people to focus on what matters most. When there is no building to maintain, no denomination to support (or submit to), and no institutional oversight, the church is unshackled to serve the Lord and reach the surrounding community. This is offered as an attempt to return to the simplicity described in Acts 2:42: "They were continually devoting themselves to the apostles' teaching and to fellowship, to the breaking of bread and to prayer." But that was a church of three thousand!

However, we need only look at the New Testament to see that life in the first-century church was anything but idyllic. Small congregations, simplified organization, and proximity to the apostles did not give the early church the spiritual advantages and insulation we might assume. In fact, we see many of the maladies that plague the church today on display in its earliest incarnations. Put simply, the purity of the early church is overrated.

And nowhere is that more apparent than in the book of Revelation.

AN APOSTLE IN EXILE

We often think of Revelation as a prophetic look at the second coming of Christ. We think of the judgment that awaits the world because "He is coming with the clouds, and every eye will see Him, even those who pierced Him; and all the tribes of the earth will mourn over Him" (Rev. 1:7). We tend to look at the promise of God's wrath in horror, but also with a sense of relief that it will not fall on us.

But before the visions of the book of Revelation reveal the subject of God's judgment against unrepentant sinners and the return of Christ, it opens with three chapters addressed to churches. Specifically, Christ dictates a message through the apostle John to the seven churches in Asia Minor: "Write in a book what you see, and send it to the seven churches: to Ephesus and to Smyrna and to Pergamum and to Thyatira and to Sardis and to Philadelphia and Laodicea" (1:11).

Those were actual congregations located in towns throughout what we know today as Turkey, listed in an order that follows the ancient postal route. Each of these churches was founded as fruit of the apostles' ministry (primarily Paul), with Ephesus serving as the mother church for all the others in that region. Toward the end of his life, John ministered in the church at Ephesus, giving him an intimate connection to all those congregations.

When the Lord revealed to him the Revelation, however, John was living in exile in a penal colony on the rocky island of Patmos.

On the night Christ was arrested, the Lord Himself had warned His disciples that persecution was coming: "If the world hates you, you know that it has hated Me before it hated you. . . . If they persecuted Me, they will also persecute you" (John 15:18, 20).

It did not take long before persecution was in full force. The church faced opposition from the very beginning, initially from Israel's religious leaders. Likewise, it endured the hostile suspicions of Rome. Roman culture was dominated by pagan and debauched religion. Christians did not fit in, nor could they partake of much that constituted everyday life in that wicked society. Moreover, Christianity simply made no sense to people steeped in Roman culture. The doctrine and practice of the early church were so utterly misunderstood that the Romans falsely accused Christians of cannibalism, incest, and other sexual perversions. Rumors spread that Christians were atheists and political dissidents because they would not worship Caesar as god. In the year AD 64, the Roman emperor Nero played on these long-held suspicions to distract from his own misdeeds. That year, when a fire devastated much of the city of Rome, the public suspected Nero was to blame. Nero shifted his deserved blame to the Christians, instituting an official campaign of persecution against them across the city and beyond. It continued throughout the rest of his reign. During that first wave of Roman persecution, both Peter and Paul were executed, along with countless others who were hunted down and slaughtered for sport.

Also during Nero's reign, Rome waged a bloody war to suppress Israel's hopes for independence. Nearly a thousand towns, villages, and settlements across Israel were burned to the ground, with their inhabitants massacred or scattered. In AD 70, Jerusalem was overthrown and the temple destroyed. What was once the capital city of God's kingdom on earth was now under the control of pagans.

Just over a decade later, Rome initiated another wave of persecution under the emperor Domitian. This second campaign against the church lasted longer—from AD 81 to 96—and extended throughout the empire. Rome's assault on the church was organized and militarized. Thousands of Christians lost their lives while others were banished or fled. Historians tell us it was during this period that Timothy was clubbed to death. Tertullian—who was born about 60 years after the apostle John died—claimed that "the Apostle John was first plunged, unhurt, into boiling oil, and thence remitted to his island-exile!"[11] Lacking firsthand witness testimony, we needn't insist on the veracity of that tradition, but it does accurately reflect the ferocity of Rome's campaign against Christians. Nero was said to smear Christians with pitch or pine resin and bind them in papyrus or bundles of wood. Or he might crucify them on crosses soaked in creosote. He would then pierce their throats so they could not scream, and set them ablaze while still alive, using them as torches to illuminate his garden parties.[12]

In Revelation 1:9, John tells us he was sentenced to the island prison of Patmos "because of the word of God and the testimony of Jesus." Preaching the gospel was a crime punishable by death. Patmos is not at all the island paradise some might initially imagine. It's actually a crescent-shaped rock jutting up out of the Aegean Sea, roughly ten miles long and five miles wide. In John's day, it was a desolate, isolated place, nearly forty miles off the coast of Miletus, between Asia Minor and Athens. John's sentence likely included the forfeiture of all his property and possessions, along with any civil rights he enjoyed under Roman law. Although he was living in exile, he was essentially given a death sentence, since he would spend the rest of his life doing hard labor in the quarries, with meager food and desperate living conditions. Already in his nineties, John could not have expected to survive for long on Patmos.

Like Paul in 2 Corinthians 11:23–29, however, the physical pain John endured could not compare to his anguish over his beloved churches in Asia Minor and their defection from the authority of God's Word. From the letters Christ dictated to the individual churches—which we will examine in greater detail in the chapters that follow—we know they were engaged in a variety of sinful behaviors, including sexual immorality, idolatry, and hypocrisy. They were tolerating sin and compromising with the pagan culture surrounding them. They willingly accommodated false teachers and even helped spread their heresy. In many ways, they were examples that would be repeated by churches in subsequent ages, including evangelical churches across the Western world today.

Twenty-five years before John's vision on Patmos, the apostle Paul warned of the dangers facing the early church. He urged Timothy, "Do not be ashamed of the testimony of our Lord or of me His prisoner, but join with me in suffering for the gospel" (2 Tim.

1:8). In verses 13–14, Paul charged him to "retain the standard of sound words which you have heard from me. . . . Guard, through the Holy Spirit who dwells in us, the treasure which has been entrusted to you."

Paul knew persecution and suffering would reach Timothy's doorstep. He also knew how easy it would be to crumble and compromise when threatened with prison, torture, and death. Throughout his final epistle, he sought to prepare his young apprentice for future trials. He continued in chapter 2:

> Be strong in the grace that is in Christ Jesus. . . . Suffer hardship with me, as a good soldier of Christ Jesus. (vv. 1, 3)

> Be diligent to present yourself approved to God as a workman who does not need to be ashamed, accurately handling the word of truth. But avoid worldly and empty chatter, for it will lead to further ungodliness, and their talk will spread like gangrene. (vv. 15–17)

> Flee from youthful lusts and pursue righteousness. . . . But refuse foolish and ignorant speculations. (vv. 22–23)

Paul's concern wasn't just for Timothy, but for the whole church. He understood the spiritual threats that loomed on the horizon for God's people:

> In the last days difficult times will come. For men will be lovers of self, lovers of money, boastful, arrogant, revilers, disobedient to parents, ungrateful, unholy, unloving, irreconcilable, malicious gossips, without self-control, brutal, haters of good, treacherous, reckless, conceited, lovers of pleasure rather than lovers of God, holding to a form of godliness, although they have denied its power;

> Avoid such men as these. . . . But evil men and imposters
> will proceed from bad to worse, deceiving and being
> deceived. (3:1–5, 14)

Throughout his ministry, the apostle Paul carefully warned about the danger of succumbing to false teachers and the need to be vigilant and discerning in the face of their threat. "Now I urge you, brethren, keep your eye on those who cause dissensions and hindrances contrary to the teaching which you learned, and turn away from them. For such men are slaves, not of our Lord Christ but of their own appetites; and by their smooth and flattering speech they deceive the hearts of the unsuspecting" (Rom. 16:17–18).

But he also understood that the fight to maintain the doctrinal and moral purity of the church is not exclusively external—that plenty of threats come from within as well: "For the time will come when they will not endure sound doctrine; but wanting to have their ears tickled, they will accumulate for themselves teachers in accordance to their own desires, and will turn away their ears from the truth and will turn aside to myths" (2 Tim. 4:3–4). As he prepared to leave the Ephesian church, Paul gave the elders there a vivid warning to guard the flock God had entrusted to them: "I know that after my departure savage wolves will come in among you, not sparing the flock; and from among your own selves men will arise, speaking perverse things, to draw away the disciples after them. Therefore be on the alert" (Acts 20:29–31). Not thirty years later, that church had drifted from their love for Christ into empty piety, while several of the surrounding congregations had succumbed to some of the very corruptions Paul warned of.

JUDGMENT FOR THE HOUSEHOLD OF GOD

By the time he reached that point in his life, John knew very well that "all who desire to live godly in Christ Jesus will be persecuted"

(2 Tim. 3:12). He told people in his pastoral care, "Do not be surprised, brethren, if the world hates you" (1 John 3:13). But as John was living out his final days in torturous labor on the Isle of Patmos, he may have looked back in amazement at how different his circumstances were from what he expected when he set out to follow Jesus.

Israel had very high expectations for the Messiah and the kingdom He would institute. They eagerly anticipated the arrival of an heir to the Davidic throne who would overthrow Rome's occupying forces, wipe out Israel's enemies, and usher in the fulfillment of all God's promises to Abraham, David, and the prophets. The salvation they awaited was temporal, not eternal.

The disciples held that hope. Throughout Christ's ministry, they frequently jockeyed for supremacy in the promised kingdom of heaven (see Matt. 18:1–5; Luke 9:46–48). John and his brother James even enlisted their mother to petition the Lord on their behalf (Matt. 20:20–21). Acts 1:6 tells us that right up to the moment Christ ascended into heaven, His disciples expected Him to unleash His sovereign power and inaugurate His kingdom on earth.

In the years that followed, as the church exploded into existence and the Holy Spirit authenticated the apostles' ministry through miraculous gifts, it must have seemed that the Lord's return was imminent. But almost immediately the church was inundated with false teachers. Before long, many of John's apostolic brothers were dead at the hands of Rome—by the time he reached Patmos, he was the only apostle still alive.

With believers on the run from merciless persecution and with churches in serious spiritual decline, John might have had every reason to be disappointed and depressed. Had the Lord's plan for the church failed? It would be easy to imagine him crying out for a vision of what the Lord was doing in His church—some divine insight to encourage and comfort him in the twilight of his apostolic ministry. No matter how seasoned and spiritually mature he was, he surely could have used some hope and solace.

Instead, what he saw was utterly terrifying. John tells us it caused him to fall to the ground "like a dead man" (Rev. 1:17). What he saw was the glorified Christ, appearing as ruler, judge, and executioner. John saw the Lord in all His glory as the Head of the church, ready to mete out righteous judgment—not on the world, but on His church!

Christ's message to the church, through John, is unequivocal: "Repent." Over and over, Christ calls these wayward churches to repent and reform. To the church at Ephesus, He said, "Therefore remember from where you have fallen, and repent and do the deeds you did at first" (Rev. 2:5). He had a similar message for the church at Pergamum: "Therefore repent; or else I am coming to you quickly, and I will make war against them with the sword of My mouth" (2:16). He warned the church at Thyatira of the severe judgment that awaited "unless they repent" (2:22). He charged the church at Sardis to "remember what you have received and heard; and keep it, and repent" (3:3). And He gave a final warning to the church at Laodicea, reminding them that "those whom I love, I reprove and discipline; therefore be zealous and repent" (3:19).

These were not casual, dispassionate warnings. Each call to repentance was accompanied by the devastating consequences that awaited if a church failed to reform. In that sense, what John saw and heard was the fulfillment of Peter's words decades earlier in his first epistle: "For it is time for judgment to begin with the household of God" (1 Peter 4:17). Like Paul, Peter knew the many looming spiritual dangers that threatened the church, even from within. He also knew that churches would in some cases succumb to temptations, false doctrines, the lure of the world, or the assaults of the Evil One. Peter called his readers to persevere under persecution, which he saw in part as God's judgment against the unfaithful church. Moreover, Peter understood that this is how God always operates with His people.

As a good student of the Old Testament, Peter would have been familiar with the prophecy of Ezekiel 9, which was another terrifying vision of God's judgment: "Then He cried out in my hearing with a loud voice saying, 'Draw near, O executioners of the city, each with his destroying weapon in his hand'" (Ezek. 9:1). Writing during the Babylonian captivity, Ezekiel saw a vision of God calling foreign powers to execute His judgment on His people. The vision continues,

> Behold, six men came from the direction of the upper gate which faces north, each with his shattering weapon in his hand; and among them was a certain man clothed in linen with a writing case at his loins. And they went in and stood beside the bronze altar.
>
> Then the glory of the God of Israel went up from the cherub on which it had been, to the threshold of the temple. And He called to the man clothed in linen at whose loins was the writing case. The LORD said to him, "Go through the midst of the city, even through the midst of Jerusalem, and put a mark on the foreheads of the men who sigh and groan over all the abominations which are being committed in its midst." But to the others He said in my hearing, "Go through the city after him and strike; do no let your eye have pity and do not spare. Utterly slay old men, young men, maidens, little children, and women, but do not touch any man on whom is the mark; and you shall start from My sanctuary." So they started with the elders who were before the temple. (vv. 2–6)

God's wrath had reached a boiling point with apostate Israel. He made a provision to mark out the few who had remained faithful, but everyone else would face the fullness of His judgment. Moreover, the slaughter would start at the very seat of His authority and the center of worship, with those most culpable for Israel's apostasy.

In essence, that is the same vision John saw—the Lord as the righteous Judge, coming to call His churches to repent of unfaithfulness to Him.

Most people who go to a church believe it is a safe place—perhaps the *safest place*—when it comes to threats of judgment from the Lord. It's almost like climbing aboard the ark; once you're safely inside, you're untouchable.

But that's not true. Frankly, it's a foolish and dangerous notion. Just because you are in a church—or something you call a church, where Jesus' name is invoked and songs are sung about Him—does not mean you're safe against threats from God. Here in the opening chapters of Revelation, the Lord makes some very strong, direct threats against churches. A church is no safer than the world in that regard, and its transgressions often demand a swifter judgment.

That's why this passage is so often overlooked and rarely discussed. While the Lord repeatedly called for Israel to repent and return to a right relationship with Him, the early chapters of Revelation are the only place He employs similar language when dealing with the sins and failures of churches. It makes us uncomfortable to think about God calling His church to repent and reform, and threatening them with judgment if they don't. But it is critically important that we heed the warnings Christ delivers to us through the pen of John in Revelation.

Yes, these were letters written to specific local congregations about their particular issues. But they also stand as warnings to the entire church throughout its history. And as we'll see, the rebukes delivered to the churches of Asia Minor are just as applicable to the modern church, if not more so.

The issues that corrupted churches in the first century are the same threats facing the church today: idolatry, sexual immorality, compromise with the world and its pagan culture, spiritual deadness, and hypocrisy. Over the intervening centuries, the church has not outgrown these familiar pitfalls. Nor has God lowered or softened His righteous standard. Regardless of when and where it exists, He demands a pure church.

That was His message to the churches in Revelation. Roughly two thousand years later, Christ is still calling churches to repent and warning us about dire consequences if they don't.

2

The Lord's Work in His Church

Before we consider the Lord's individual letters to the churches of Asia Minor, we need to pay careful attention to what John saw in his vision of the glorified Christ. Don't miss the significance of how the Lord chose to manifest His glory and pull back the curtain on His ongoing work in the church. There are no meaningless details included here. Everything John saw helped inform and illuminate Christ's call for the church to repent.

John begins the description of his vision in Revelation 1:9. Rather than asserting his apostolic authority, he humbly identifies himself as "your brother and fellow partaker in the tribulation and kingdom and perseverance which are in Jesus." As a redeemed man, he's in the kingdom. His faith has endured, so he is marked by perseverance. But he's in the midst of persecution, living in exile "because of the word of God and the testimony of Jesus." It was a high crime to preach the gospel. By now, all the other apostles are dead. Believers are being hunted down and killed. Worst of all, the church is defecting from the truth, abandoning the faithful teaching that John and the apostles delivered to them. It's a bleak time in the life of the church. That likely made John's vision all the more stunning.

He continues,

> I was in the Spirit on the Lord's day, and I heard behind me a loud voice like the sound of a trumpet, saying, "Write in a book what you see, and send it to the seven churches: to Ephesus and to Smyrna and to Pergamum and to Thyatira and to Sardis and to Philadelphia and to Laodicea."
>
> Then I turned to see the voice that was speaking with me. And having turned I saw seven golden lampstands; and in the middle of the lampstands I saw one like a son of man, clothed in a robe reaching to the feet, and girded across His chest with a golden sash. His head and His hair were white like white wool, like snow; and His eyes were like a flame of fire. His feet were like burnished bronze, when it has been made to glow in a furnace, and His voice was like the sound of many waters. In His right hand He held seven stars, and out of His mouth came a sharp two-edged sword; and His face was like the sun shining in its strength.
>
> When I saw Him, I fell at His feet like a dead man. And He placed His right hand on me, saying, "Do not be afraid; I am the first and the last, and the living One; and I was dead, and behold, I am alive forevermore, and I have the keys of death and of Hades. Therefore, write the things which you have seen, and the things which are, and the things which will take place after these things. As for the mystery of the seven stars which you saw in My right hand, and the seven golden lampstands: the

seven stars are the angels of the seven churches, and the seven lampstands are the seven churches. (vv. 10–20)

All the elements of John's vision carry powerful doctrinal implications for the church's relationship with Christ, its Head. No other text of Scripture offers such vivid and comprehensive insight into what the Lord is doing in His church—not only in the congregations of Asia Minor, but throughout the entire history of the body of Christ.

A VOICE LIKE A TRUMPET

John doesn't spend much time setting the scene of his vision. Two details will suffice: "I was in the Spirit on the Lord's day" (1:10). The phrase "in the Spirit" simply signifies that this was not a normal, human experience. Through the Holy Spirit, John was empowered to experience something outside his senses, and outside the physical realm. John's vision cannot be explained by any phenomena of the created world—he wasn't sleeping or dreaming; he is wide awake. Perfectly coherent and in his right mind, John was transported by the Spirit beyond the limits of human understanding to a spiritual plane of existence where he could commune directly with God.

This is exceedingly rare, even for an apostle, but Scripture does indicate some other instances of similar supernatural experiences. Isaiah "saw the Lord sitting on a throne, lofty and exalted, with the train of His robe filling the temple" (Isa. 6:1). Ezekiel writes of how "the Spirit entered me and set me on my feet; and I heard Him speaking to me" (Ezek. 2:2). The book of Acts describes similar visions from the Lord for both Peter (10:9–16) and Paul (22:17–21). Concerning his own supernatural experience, Paul would later write to the Corinthians, "I know a man in Christ who fourteen years ago—whether in the body I do not know, or out of the body I do not know, God knows—such a man was caught up to the third heaven. And I know how such a man—whether in the body or apart I do not know, God knows—was caught up into Paradise and heard inexpressible words, which a man is not permitted to speak" (2 Cor. 12:2–4).

Like Paul, we can't say for certain *how* it happened for John. What we know is that the Lord supernaturally opened John's awareness to the divine realm to communicate clearly and vividly with him; and through him, to us.

The only other detail John gives us is that he received this vision "on the Lord's day" (Rev. 1:10). This is not an eschatological designation. John is not referring here to the Day of the Lord and God's return in judgment (see 2 Peter 3:10). By the end of the first century, "the Lord's day" was the customary way for Christians to refer to the first day of the week—to memorialize the day the Lord rose from the grave. John is simply telling us it was a Sunday on Patmos.

On that particular Sunday, John says he "heard behind me a loud voice like the sound of a trumpet" (1:10). The Old Testament refers to a similar sound before God delivered His Law to the Israelites at Sinai: "So it came about on the third day, when it was morning, that there were thunder and lightning flashes and a thick cloud upon the mountain and a very loud trumpet sound, so that all the people who were in the camp trembled" (Ex. 19:16).

Throughout the book of Revelation, a loud sound or voice precedes solemn announcements and expressions of heavenly praise (see 8:13; 14:2). It's a piercing, penetrating sound. It's a sound like a trumpet, but it doesn't come from an instrument. In John's vision, it's the voice of the Lord Himself, instantly commanding the apostle's full attention and drowning out any other noise. The sound is unmistakable—the risen, glorified Lord Jesus Christ is speaking. It's time to listen.

And what did He say? "Write in a book what you see, and send it to the seven churches: to Ephesus and to Smyrna and to Pergamum and to Thyatira and to Sardis and to Philadelphia and to Laodicea" (Rev. 1:11).

Suffering in exile, it's possible that John wondered why the Lord had kept him alive. Why hadn't he been put to death like the rest of the apostles? Why did he live long enough to see the church slip into spiritual decline? Was there even a future for the church?

In verse 11, God gives him the answer. The Lord still had more work for him to do. He still had one book left to write. He receives the privilege of looking ahead to the end of time—to the final victory over sin and the future glorification of the church. Doomed to a rock of exile, the apostle soared on the wings of prophetic revelation to the very throne of God and the glory of Christ. Shut out from the world, he would now traverse the heavens.

The Lord tells him to write what he sees. And what he saw was incredible.

THE LORD IN HIS CHURCH

John writes, "Then I turned to see the voice that was speaking with me. And having turned I saw seven golden lampstands" (1:12). Lamps in the ancient world were commonly made out of clay or metal. They were filled with oil and a floating wick. But left down low they did not produce much light. To illuminate a full room, you needed to elevate them on a lampstand. Such lampstands would have been familiar to John's readers in the first century. However, the lampstands John saw would have been unlike any they had seen before, made out of pure gold. Such costly material immediately indicates the tremendous value of these lampstands.

In verse 20, Jesus explains the significance of these valuable items: "As for the mystery of . . . the seven golden lampstands: the seven . . . lampstands are the seven churches." Just as a lampstand was used to illuminate a room, God has called His church to be the lights of the world (Phil. 2:15). That they are made out of gold shows how precious the church is to God. In fact, there is nothing more valuable on earth, and nothing that was bought at so high a price (Acts 20:28).

John identifies the seven churches as those mentioned in verse 11. But the imagery is not limited to them alone. In Scripture, the number seven often signifies completeness. So while these specific churches will receive specific messages from God, His words are nonetheless valid for the entire church. In John's vision, they stand as distinct churches and symbolize the church throughout its history in all its variations.

That's not all. John says, "And in the middle of the lampstands I saw one like a son of man" (Rev. 1:13). This is Christ Himself, the Son of Man. But He does not appear like the Christ John last saw before the ascension. At the end of His ministry, Christ's full glory was still cloaked in His resurrected body. Here in John's vision, it is now on full display.

There's a tremendous comfort and encouragement in the depiction of Christ in the midst of His church. John would have remembered the promise the Lord made to His disciples on the night of His arrest. "I will not leave you as orphans; I will come to you" (John 14:18). As He departed this earth, Christ comforted His disciples, "I am with you always, even to the end of the age" (Matt. 28:20). The author of Hebrews included that reminder for the New Testament church, quoting God's repeated promise to Israel: "I will never desert you, nor will I ever forsake you" (Heb. 13:5). John knew the Lord would not abandon him or the church. But this visual reminder of the Lord's constant communion with His own was nevertheless a welcome reassurance and encouragement.

It should encourage us, as well. We don't serve a distant god or an ancient martyr. The Lord of the church is alive and active in the midst of His people. And the subsequent details of John's vision give us insight into exactly what Christ is doing in His church.

THE INTERCEDING HIGH PRIEST

John describes Christ's appearance in Revelation 1:13, saying He was "clothed in a robe reaching to the feet, and girded across His chest with a golden sash." The robe John describes could indicate majesty or official rank—certainly, Christ is the preeminent One in the church. Earlier in his introductory salutations, John did identify Christ as "the ruler of the kings of the earth" (1:5).

But the language John uses to describe the robe and particularly the golden sash is directly tied to the garments worn by Israel's high priest (see Lev. 16:4). What John sees is a depiction of Christ in His role as the Great High Priest, interceding on behalf of His church.

The writer of Hebrews repeatedly extolls Christ's work as our Great High Priest, who is "able to save forever those who draw near to God through Him, since He always lives to make intercession for them" (Heb. 7:25). "But when Christ appeared as a high priest of the good things to come, He entered through the greater and more perfect tabernacle, not made with hands, that is to say, not of this creation; and not through the blood of goats and calves, but through His own blood, He entered the holy place once for all, having obtained eternal redemption" (9:11–12). He is "a merciful and faithful high priest in things pertaining to God, [able] to make propitiation for the sins of the people" (2:17). As our High Priest, Christ is unparalleled in His capacity to sympathize with our weakness (4:15), and "He is able to come to the aid of those who are tempted" (2:18).

In Romans 8, Paul extolls the blessings of Christ's priestly work: "Who will bring a charge against God's elect? God is the one who justifies; who is the one who condemns? Christ Jesus is He who died, yes, rather who was raised, who is at the right hand of God, who also intercedes for us" (vv. 33–34). He goes on to explain that our relationship with God is impervious to assault—that because of Christ's intercessory work, nothing can separate us from His love (vv. 38–39).

Again, this is a tremendous comfort for believers—our Savior lives, and He is perpetually working in His church, interceding on our behalf and sympathetically moving for His glory and our good.

THE PURIFYING SOVEREIGN

It's not merely Christ's priestly garb that evidences His work in His church. John continues in Revelation 1:14, "His head and His hair were white like white wool, like snow." Christ's head and His hair weren't just white—they gleamed in blazing, brilliant white, like the purest wool and snow. John's word choice here is telling—he's referencing Daniel 7:9, which describes the Ancient of Days seated on His throne, and "the hair of His head like pure wool." The imagery here not only affirms Christ's deity, but also speaks to His purity. He is utterly unblemished and absolutely holy.

He expects His people to be holy as well. As Paul explained to the Ephesians, that was the Lord's purpose in saving them in the first place. He says Christ "loved the church and gave Himself up for her, so that He might sanctify her, having cleansed her by the washing of water with the word, that He might present to Himself the church in all her glory, having no spot or wrinkle or any such thing; but that she would be holy and blameless" (Eph. 5:25–27). He likewise exhorted the Colossians, reminding them that Christ "has now reconciled you in His fleshly body through death, in order to present you before Him holy and blameless and beyond reproach" (Col. 1:22). Peter put it bluntly in his first epistle: "Like the Holy One who called you, be holy yourselves also in all your behavior; because it is written, 'You shall be holy, for I am holy'" (1 Peter 1:15–16). During the Sermon on the Mount, Christ Himself declared, "You are to be perfect, as your heavenly Father is perfect" (Matt. 5:48).

Given everything Scripture tells us about the purity and holiness of the Lord, I cannot understand how professing believers live the kind of lives they live; or how so-called churches can operate the way they do—the repeated dalliances with sin, the unending attempts to curry favor with unrepentant sinners. Too many people in the church today live in blatant disregard for the apostle James's stark warning: "You adulteresses, do you not know that friendship with the world is hostility toward God? Therefore whoever wishes to be a friend of the world makes himself an enemy of God" (James 4:4). The constant affront to Christ's holiness from those who should know better is heartbreaking. John must have felt that way with regard to the churches in Asia Minor.

And his vision illustrates that no matter what is going on in the church, the Lord Himself is fully aware. The apostle writes, "His eyes were like a flame of fire" (Rev. 1:14). It's a picture of Christ's holy omniscience. Like penetrating lasers, the eyes of the Lord see everything. Nothing escapes His notice; no secret remains hidden. His piercing gaze sees right to the heart of His church, and into the heart of every believer.

Matthew 10:26 tells us, "There is nothing concealed that will not be revealed, or hidden that will not be known." The author of Hebrews explains the comprehensive nature of the Lord's omniscience: "There is no creature hidden from His sight, but all things are open and laid bare to the eyes of Him with whom we have to do" (Heb. 4:13). The Lord of the church will not fail to recognize sin in His church.

Nor will He fail to deal with it. John's vision continues in Revelation 1:15: "His feet were like burnished bronze, when it has been made to glow in a furnace." In the ancient world, kings and rulers sat on elevated thrones, so that those under their authority were kept under their feet. In that sense, a king's feet symbolized his authority and judgment. But unlike human rulers made of flesh, our Lord has feet of burnished bronze—blazing, molten feet of judgment. John sees Christ moving in His church not just as its High Priest, but also as its King and Judge.

This is not the final judgment against sin, but of Christ's pruning, purging work within His church. For the sake of the church's purity, He will discipline His own. Christ spoke of this very thing in John's gospel: "Every branch in Me that does not bear fruit, He takes away; and every branch that bears fruit, He prunes it so that it may bear more fruit" (John 15:2).

The writer of Hebrews went into greater detail:

> You have forgotten the exhortation which is addressed to you as sons, "My son, do not regard lightly the discipline of the Lord, nor faint when you are reproved by Him; for those whom the Lord loves He disciplines, and He scourges every son whom He receives." It is for discipline that you endure; God deals with you as with sons; for what son is there whom his father does not discipline? But if you are without discipline, of which all have become partakers, then you are illegitimate children and not sons. Furthermore, we had earthly fathers to discipline us, and we respected them; shall we not much rather be subject to the Father of spirits, and live? For they disciplined us for a short time as seemed best to them, but He disciplines us for our good, so that we may share His holiness.
> (HEB. 12:5–10)

The Lord loves His church enough to discipline it, to bring the necessary chastisement to protect its purity. And through His Word, He instructs us how we are to guard its purity. Matthew 18 lays out the prescription for dealing with sin in the church—a pattern the church today largely ignores to its own hurt. Scripture warns us of the dire consequences if we fail to protect the purity of God's church. In Acts 5, Ananias and Sapphira were struck dead in the middle of a congregational meeting for lying to the Holy Spirit and the church. In 1 Corinthians 11, Paul tells us that some in the Corinthian church were sick because they carelessly celebrated the Lord's Supper, while others had died.

When you see a believer whose life is crushed because of sin, or a church leader who is forced out of ministry because of secret corruption in his life, you're seeing the Lord at work in His church. He intercedes to protect His own, but He also purifies the church by disciplining His own.

THE VOICE OF AUTHORITY

The next feature of John's vision does not deal with what John saw, but rather with what he heard. In Revelation 1:15, he writes, "And His voice was like the sound of many waters." There are no soft, sandy beaches on the Isle of Patmos; no gentle, soothing tide. During a storm, the waves crash against the rocks with a deafening roar. That violent, arresting sound was how John described the voice of the Lord. It's an echo of Ezekiel 43:2, affirming that Christ and the Father speak with the same thundering voice of authority over the church.

John had heard this voice before. At Christ's transfiguration, the voice of God rang out, saying, "This is My Son, My Chosen One; listen to Him!" (Luke 9:35). One of the defining characteristics of believers is that they recognize the authority of Christ and obey His Word: "My sheep hear My voice, and I know them, and they follow Me" (John 10:27). Submitting to the authority of Christ is fundamental to the life of faith: "If you love Me, you will keep My commandments" (John 14:15).

I frequently hear pastors say, "You need to learn to listen to the voice of God. You need to be tuned in so you can hear His still, small voice." I have no idea what that means. God does not mumble. He doesn't whisper gentle niceties into the ears of His people. When the Lord speaks to His church, it is unmistakable.

His voice thunders over the church through the divine authority of Holy Scripture.

DIVINE CARE AND PROTECTION

Not only does the Lord speak with authority over His church, He exercises sovereign control over it. In Revelation 1:16, John sees that Christ is holding something in His hand: "In His right hand He held seven stars." In verse 20, Jesus clarifies who these stars represent: "The seven stars are the angels of the seven churches."

That common translation has led to significant confusion and disagreement among scholars and commentators. It's true that the word *angeloi* can mean angels—but think through the implications of that reading. Why would Christ give John a message to be relayed to angels who would then deliver it to the church? The Lord certainly could find a less circuitous means of communication with His heavenly host. Moreover, Scripture never gives angels authority over the church. Hebrews 1:14 describes them as ministering servants, not leaders.

John's explanation in verse 20 makes much simpler and clearer sense if we read *angeloi* as "messengers," as it is translated elsewhere (see Luke 7:24; 9:52; James 2:25). In that sense, then, John is most likely referring to pastors or leaders from each of the seven churches. It's entirely possible that John was able to receive visitors, and that these men would carry God's Word back to their churches. (We know someone performed that function. How else would we be reading Revelation today?)

Scripture doesn't tell us who these men were specifically, but the message of John's vision is clear: the Lord will always have His chosen shepherds. What a great comfort it is that He holds them in the palm of His hand.

As we'll see, the situation in Asia Minor was bleak. Spiritual defection was well underway in some of these congregations. Persecution had come—some had fled, and others compromised with the world. But in the midst of it all, the Lord still had His faithful men serving in His church.

The same is true throughout every generation of the church. It's easy to get discouraged when we see weak, foolish pastors leading their churches astray, when there is a noticeable absence of godly leadership. It's all the more heart-rending when an unfaithful shepherd makes a shipwreck of his faith through immorality and ungodliness. We're right to be grieved when hirelings and false teachers make a mockery of the gospel. But we must not forget that the church is always under the sovereign care of Christ. He will always have faithful shepherds that He gifts, calls, and sets apart to care for His sheep.

Further, He will not ignore those who bring a blight upon His church through wickedness and false teaching. John's vision continues in Revelation 1:16 with an illustration of the Lord's sovereign protection for His church. He writes, "And out of His mouth came a sharp two-edged sword." This is no dainty dagger. This is the devastating broadsword of God's truth. Later in Revelation, God will deploy it against the ungodly (19:15, 21). But here, the Lord is wielding it in judgment against enemies and threats within the church. In His letter to the church at Pergamum—a church overrun with heresy and false teachers—Christ warns, "I am coming to you quickly, and I will make war against them with the sword of my mouth" (2:16). He uses the sword of His truth to prune away any threats to the purity of His church.

Hebrews 4:12 reminds us of the lethal potency of God's truth: "For the word of God is living and active and sharper than any two-edged sword, and piercing as far as the division of soul and spirit, of both joints and marrow, and able to judge the thoughts and intentions of the heart." This is the Lord's weapon of choice against deceivers, charlatans, and every false teacher who makes mockery or merchandise of His gospel. He wields the sword of

His Word against the enemies of His people so that nothing will prevent Him from building His church (Matt. 16:18).

A REFLECTION OF GLORY

John gives us one final detail about the appearance of Christ in Revelation 1:16: "and His face was like the sun shining in its strength." Looking at the Lord's face was like staring directly into the sun at high noon on a clear day. What was this blazing light? It's the *shekinah*—the brilliant, holy glory of God, radiating in the face of His Son.

It appears John borrowed this expression from Judges 5:31, which says, "Let those who love Him be like the rising of the sun in its might." Matthew 13:43 echoes the idea: "The righteous will shine forth as the sun in the kingdom of their Father." The glory of God, in the person of Jesus Christ, shines through the church, and thus the people of God reflect His glory to a watching world. Paul makes that very point in 2 Corinthians 4:6: "For God, who said, 'Light shall shine out of darkness,' is the One who has shone in our hearts to give the Light of the knowledge of the glory of God in the face of Christ."

Through the transformed lives of His people, the Lord is making the gospel attractive to the unrepentant world. He is drawing men and women to Himself through the godly character of His church. Christ Himself established that very pattern in Matthew's gospel: "Let your light shine before men in such a way that they may see your good works, and glorify your Father who is in heaven" (Matt. 5:16).

This is the climactic reality of the church: God redeems sinners to build His church and uses their transformed lives to reflect the majesty of His glory, whereby He draws more sinners to Himself. The awesome, blazing glory of the Lord shines through the church, illuminating a lost and dark world.

TERROR TURNS TO COMFORT

What is the appropriate response to this vivid depiction of Christ's work in His church? John collapsed "like a dead man" at the Lord's feet (Rev. 1:17). Throughout Scripture, that kind of intense, overwhelming fear was the consistent reaction of everyone who experienced a heavenly vision or encounter. When the Angel of the Lord appeared and announced the birth of Samson, "Manoah said to his wife, 'We shall surely die, for we have seen God'" (Judg. 13:22). Overwhelmed at his vision of God in the temple, Isaiah cried, "Woe is me, for I am ruined! Because I am a man of unclean lips, and I live among a people of unclean lips; for my eyes have seen the King, the LORD of hosts" (Isa. 6:5). After an angel appeared to him, Daniel writes, "My natural color turned to a deathly pallor, and I retained no strength" (Dan. 10:8). At the sight of a bright light from heaven on the road to Damascus, Saul of Tarsus and his traveling companions collapsed to the ground (Acts 26:13–14). John, along with Peter and James, fell to the ground at the sound of God's voice during Christ's transfiguration (Matt. 17:6). And one day, the unrepentant world will realize the terror of God's judgment and call out "to the mountains and to the rocks, 'Fall on us and hide us from the presence of Him who sits on the throne, and from the wrath of the Lamb; for the great day of their wrath has come, and who is able to stand?'" (Rev. 6:16–17).

Scripture is clear: unlike the frivolous, boastful accounts of men and women today who falsely claim to have seen God, the immediate response from everyone who genuinely saw the Lord was fear. Sinners—even redeemed sinners—are right to be terrified in the presence of a Holy God. There is always fear in a true vision of Christ, because we see His glory and He sees our sin.

John crumbled at the trauma of his vision. In the presence of the Lord, staring at His bronze feet of judgment and the double-edged sword of His Word, we would likewise collapse in a lifeless heap.

But that terror turned to comfort and assurance as the vision continued: "He placed His right hand on me, saying 'Do not be afraid; I am the first and the last, and the living One; and I was dead, and behold, I am alive forevermore, and I have the keys of death and of Hades'" (vv. 17–18).

Those simple words delivered a powerful message of tremendous encouragement for John, and for all believers: the Lord is not our executioner. Although Christ administers chastening and judgment against the church, the debt for our sins has already been paid. He "was dead" and is "alive forevermore." That simple truth should perpetually buoy our hearts in grateful assurance of our salvation. John proclaimed this great assurance in his opening salutation: Christ "loves us and released us from our sins by His blood" (v. 5). Christ alone holds "the keys of death and of Hades." The redeemed have nothing to fear. Jesus proclaims, "I am the resurrection and the life; he who believes in Me will live even if he dies, and everyone who lives and believes in Me will never die" (John 11:25–26). This was the assurance and comfort He brought to John in the midst of his fear: Your debt has already been paid. You belong to me, and nothing—not even your sin—can change that.

John had not misinterpreted his vision; Christ *was* moving in judgment against His church. But the righteous Judge was not coming for John. He had work for His beloved apostle to accomplish. He said, "Therefore write the things which you have seen, and the things which are, and the things which will take place after these things" (Rev. 1:19). John's commission was not yet complete. He had a duty to record what he had already seen, what the Lord still had to say to the churches of Asia Minor, and the prophetic visions that unfold throughout the remainder of the book. In other words, "Pick yourself up. Dust yourself off. And get to work."

That same assurance and encouragement extends to every believer. The initial terror of seeing God move in judgment against His church turns to comfort when we reflect on what He has done for us. We don't have anything to fear because Christ has died and risen again for us. He has redeemed us, and He is always interceding for us, protecting our purity, and providing faithful shepherds to guard His flock. Amazingly, in spite of our unworthiness, He has work for us to accomplish. We're not going to write another book of the Bible. But we have been called to proclaim the glory of His gospel to the ends of the earth. It's time to get to work.

3

The Loveless Church
EPHESUS

In an attempt to back Jesus into a doctrinal corner, the Pharisees challenged Him to identify the most important commandment in the Law of God (Matt. 22:36). He responded, "'You shall love the Lord your God with all your heart, and with all your soul, and with all your mind.' This is the great and foremost commandment" (vv. 37–38; see also Luke 10:27).

Our love for the Lord is the truest measure of our commitment to Him. He made that point to His disciples in John 14, saying, "He who has My commandments and keeps them is the one who loves Me; and he who loves Me will be loved by My Father, and I will love him and disclose Myself to him. . . . If anyone loves Me, he will keep My word" (vv. 21, 23). To expose the true nature of Peter's heart, the Lord asked him three times, "Do you love Me?" (John 21:15–17). Christ demands our undivided love: "He who loves father or mother more than Me is not worthy of Me; and he who loves son or daughter more than Me is not worthy of Me" (Matt. 10:37). The mark of true children of God is that they love

His Son (John 8:42). Paul said that the love of Christ controls His people (2 Cor. 5:14).

Put simply, loving Christ is the defining characteristic of a Christian. And while the genuine believer will always love the Lord, the intensity of his love can fluctuate over time. The redeemed person's love for Christ must be carefully guarded and nurtured, or it will diminish with time.

The truth is, none of us can ever say our love for Him really is everything it should be. That first and greatest of all the commandments—to love the Lord with all our heart, soul, strength, and mind—sets an impossibly high standard. Given the weakness of our flesh, the curse of sin, the persistence of temptation, and the many earthly distractions that vie for our attention and affections, whole-hearted, single-minded love for Christ is frustratingly elusive. We all must confess with the apostle Paul that under the standard set by the law, we are abject failures: "I find then the principle that evil is present in me, the one who wants to do good. For I joyfully concur with the law of God in the inner man, but I see a different law in the members of my body, waging war against the law of my mind and making me a prisoner of the law of sin which is in my members" (Rom. 7:21–23). "The willing is present in me, but the doing of the good is not" (v. 18).

In short, none of us has ever perfectly fulfilled the first, most basic of all God's commandments for as much as an hour. We need to recognize that failure as sin, and as the gateway to greater sin.

But our inability to fulfill God's commandment perfectly does not in any way absolve us from the duty of pursuing the standard it sets. Greater love for Christ should still be the goal of every believing heart. And we must faithfully guard against distractions and temptations that divide our hearts and diminish our love for Christ. To neglect this duty is to court spiritual disaster.

In all of Scripture, there is no better illustration of the severe dangers of declining love for God than Christ's letter to the church at Ephesus.

AN ISLAND IN A SEA OF PAGANISM

Asia Minor was utterly pagan. Even before the Roman persecution, it would have been a difficult place to minister the gospel. It was a culture dominated by worldliness, debauchery, mysticism, and idolatry. And at the center of it sat Ephesus. While Pergamum was the capital city of the region, Ephesus was its true center. Home to as many as 500,000 people, it was called the "Light of Asia," and it dominated the region.

To begin with, it was home to the primary harbor in Asia Minor, serving as the entry point for people and goods to the rest of the province. The harbor sat at the mouth of the Cayster River, roughly three miles from the city. Today it is gone; buried under miles of silt that eroded from the Cayster and filled the harbor (this likely contributed to the death of the ancient city, which today lies in ruins). In addition to its value as a shipping port, Ephesus also sat at the convergence of four major Roman trade routes. The city wasn't merely the Light of Asia; it was also its marketplace. If you were traveling through that part of the world, you went through Ephesus.

That meant the city was also a center of culture and entertainment. The theater could hold as many as 25,000 people, and every spring they hosted sporting events that rivaled the ancient Olympics. It was a massive, sprawling pageant of athletics, drama, parades, and pagan sacrifices. It's possible Paul was referring to the Ephesian Games in 1 Corinthians 16:8–9, when he writes of his plans to "remain in Ephesus until Pentecost; for a wide door for effective service has opened to me, and there are many adversaries." The influx of pilgrims and spectators from all over the Mediterranean world would have made an inviting mission field.

However, what truly set Ephesus apart was the Temple of Artemis. One of the Seven Wonders of the Ancient World, it was built out of gleaming marble and roughly the size of a full city block. It dominated not just the landscape, but the entire life of the city. In addition to its religious uses, the temple served as a museum, a vast marketplace, a bank for the wealthiest families in Asia Minor, and even a sanctuary for criminals.

But the primary function of the temple was the worship of Artemis (or Diana), the most sacred goddess in the ancient Greco-Roman world. Every day, the temple was overrun with thousands of priests, eunuchs, temple prostitutes, musicians, dancers, and other worshipers. The worship itself consisted of chaotic hysteria: drunkenness, debauchery, sexual deviance, and frenzies of self-mutilation. It was a horrific, disgusting display.

Heraclitus was a pagan Greek philosopher who was born and lived in Ephesus in the fifth-century BC, and even he was aghast at the perversions on display in his native city. He described the culture there as dark and vile, and said the morals of his fellow citizens were lower than animals. "The Ephesians deserve to be hanged, every last one of them," he wrote.[1] With such dominating spiritual darkness and corruption, Ephesus is likely not the first place you would choose to plant a church.

And yet the gospel thrived there—more than that, it exploded from that city across all of Asia Minor.

It's possible that no church in history enjoyed a stronger lineage of faithful leaders than the Ephesians were blessed to have. The book of Acts indicates that Paul's partners in ministry, Priscilla and Aquila, were the first ones to bring the gospel to the city (Acts 18:18–19). It's likely that under their leadership, the church was founded. They were soon joined by a man named Apollos—a Jew from Egypt who was "mighty in the Scriptures" (the Old Testament) and "fervent in the Spirit" (vv. 24–25). When Priscilla and Aquila heard him preaching in the synagogue, they realized he was "acquainted only with the baptism of John" (v. 25)—that is, he was still preaching the message of John the Baptist. It was Priscilla and Aquila who first told him about Jesus Christ (v. 26). In Acts 19, Paul returns to Ephesus and meets up with more disciples of John the

Baptist, whom he then led to faith in Christ (vv. 1–7). These believers were the foundation that the Ephesian church was built on.

Paul stayed in Ephesus for three years, faithfully preaching and growing the church. Acts 19:10 tells us that through his ministry, "all who lived in Asia heard the word of the Lord, both Jews and Greeks." Because of the strategic location of Ephesus, the gospel spread out in every direction. It was during this period that the other churches across Asia Minor were planted along the ancient postal route, as the gospel poured out of Ephesus.

Scripture tells us that in those days, "God was performing extraordinary miracles by the hands of Paul, so that handkerchiefs or aprons were even carried from his body to the sick, and the diseases left them and the evil spirits went out" (Acts 19:11–12). The Holy Spirit verified the message and the power of the gospel through these miraculous works. Acts indicates that some of the local exorcists were jealous of Paul's power and tried to harness it for themselves (v. 13). One group, the sons of Sceva, invoked the names of Paul and the Lord to call an evil spirit out of a man. The spirit replied, "I recognize Jesus, and I know about Paul, but who are you?" (v. 14–15). The story continues, "And the man, in whom was the evil spirit, leaped on them and subdued all of them and overpowered them, so that they fled out of that house naked and wounded" (v. 16). That's about as bad as it gets for a false exorcist. The Bible says these incidents left the entire city in the holy fear of God—that the Lord's name was magnified and His Word prevailed (vv. 17, 20).

The growing fear of the Lord put a significant dent in the consuming idolatry of the city—particularly on the business side. "Those who practiced magic brought their books together and began burning them in the sight of everyone; and they counted up the price of them and found it fifty thousand pieces of silver" (v. 19). A silversmith named Demetrius incited a riot with his fellow tradesman because the progress of the gospel was killing off the sale of the idols they fashioned (vv. 21–41). The church was exploding at such a pace that they feared the worship in the Temple of Artemis would stop altogether.

In the middle of this ancient city devoted to reprehensible paganism and vile perversion, a small group of men and women huddled together and faithfully proclaimed the message of Jesus Christ. And in spite of their environment, some of the greatest victories ever won by the gospel of grace were won in the city of Ephesus. The church flourished—first under Paul and then under Timothy (1 Tim. 1:3), Onesiphorus (2 Tim. 1:16, 18), Tychicus (2 Tim. 4:12), and finally John. No church in history could claim such a rich heritage of faithful pastors.

But as we'll see, even that unrivaled heritage could not keep them from falling into sin.

SALUTATIONS AND COMMENDATIONS

It wasn't only bad news for the Ephesian church. In fact, the Lord identifies several commendable features of their faith and service.

Revelation 2:1 says, "To the angel of the church in Ephesus write: The One who holds the seven stars in His right hand, the One who walks among the seven golden lampstands, says this." There would be no mistakes or confusion about whom this letter came from. While it was hand-delivered by men from the pen of John, the Lord unquestionably identifies Himself as its author. These are His direct, authoritative words.

He says, "I know your deeds and your toil and perseverance, and that you cannot tolerate evil men, and you put to the test those who call themselves apostles, and they are not, and you found them to be false; and you have perseverance and have endured for My name's sake, and have not grown weary" (vv. 2–3). That's a church mature Christians would eagerly join. The Lord gives them a rich and detailed commendation that speaks to their pattern of faithfulness. He says, "I know your deeds and your toil." The Greek word translated "toil" is *kopos*. It speaks of labor to the point of exhaustion; the kind of work that drains you not just physically, but emotionally and spiritually. This was a church that toiled for the sake of the kingdom and fully expended themselves for the gospel. They weren't lazy or indifferent; they were busy, giving everything they had for the cause of Christ.

The diligent Ephesians are a sharp contrast to many people today who think of church as little more than a theater, meant for their amusement and gratification. Many modern churches are full of spectators. The Ephesian church was nothing like that. They understood they had been called to hard toil in the work of God's kingdom. And they were happy to expend themselves for the sake of the gospel.

But the Ephesians were not only known for their deeds. Christ also commends their perseverance in verse 2. This is not some kind of grim resignation, or a dogged refusal to give up. The Greek word here (*hupomonē*) literally means "to remain under." It's speaking of the noble courage that readily accepts hardship, suffering, loss, and persecution. It's an invincible attitude that eagerly persists in the face of difficulties and opposition.

Verse 2 continues to describe their godly credentials, noting that they "cannot tolerate evil men." The Ephesians were sensitive to sin and the presence of evil. They hated evil as God hates evil, and recognized the damage that sin does to the fellowship and the testimony of God's church. The implication here is that they understood that "a little leaven leavens the whole lump of dough" (Gal. 5:9). It seems they followed Christ's instructions for church discipline (Matt. 18:15–20) and didn't turn a blind eye to sin in their midst. In his epistle to the church, Paul exhorted the Ephesians, "Do not give the devil an opportunity" (Eph. 4:27). Christ's words here in Revelation indicate that they faithfully guarded against Satan's attempts to infiltrate their fellowship.

They were also a church that exhibited great discernment. Revelation 2:2 notes that the Ephesians "put to the test those who call themselves apostles, and they are not, and you found them to be false."

From the outset, the early church was under assault from false teachers. The Judaizers and their legalism; the Gnostics and their elevated, secret knowledge; the Antinomians and their licentiousness—false gospels and heresies abounded in the first-century world. In his second epistle—which was likely written in Ephesus—John warned believers: "many deceivers have gone out into the world. . . . If anyone comes to you and does not bring this teaching, do not receive him into your house, and do not give him a greeting" (2 John 1:7, 10). Christ identified the threat posed by false teachers in the Sermon on the Mount: "Beware of the false prophets, who come to you in sheep's clothing, but inwardly are ravenous wolves" (Matt. 7:15). As Paul prepared to leave the Ephesian believers in Acts 20, he issued a grave warning to the elders: "I know that after my departure savage wolves will come in among you, not sparing the flock; and from among your own selves men will arise, speaking perverse things, to draw away the disciples after them. Therefore be on the alert, remembering that night and day for a period of three years I did not cease to admonish each of you with tears" (Acts 20:29–31). The believers in Ephesus took those warnings seriously and carefully "put to the test" anyone who claimed to speak for the Lord.

Revelation 2:6 also celebrates their discernment: "Yet this you do have, that you hate the deeds of the Nicolaitans, which I also hate." The nature of the Nicolaitan heresy has been lost to history; we don't know with certainty what they taught or why the Lord hated their deeds. They are mentioned again in the letter to the church at Pergamum, where their false teaching is linked with the idolatry of Balaam, perhaps indicating that their worship included idolatry and sexual immorality. What little else we know comes to us from the writing of the early church fathers. Irenaeus recorded that the Nicolaitans "lived lives of unrestrained indulgence,"[2] while Clement of Alexandria said they "[abandon] themselves to pleasure like goats, as if insulting the body, [and they] lead a life of self-indulgence."[3] Regardless of what "the deeds of the Nicolaitans" involved, the Ephesians had the godly discernment to avoid their corrupting influence. They were right to hate the heresy of the Nicolaitans; God did, too.

Where did they get such commendable discernment? From being well versed in God's truth. This was a very well-taught church. They sat under the tutelage of some of the sharpest and most godly minds in the early church. But they didn't rest on that legacy; they didn't assume their heritage alone would protect them. They put into practice the principles and doctrines handed down to them, and they faithfully guarded the church from the constant onslaught of false teaching. The modern church needs to take note of this example. You cannot defend the faith by simply asserting your credentials. Doctrinal discernment is hard work, but the legacy of a pure and protected church is one of the greatest offerings we can give to God.

Finally, the Lord sums up His commendation of the Ephesian church in verse 3: "You have perseverance and have endured for My name's sake, and have not grown weary." The key here is their motivation. For decades, they toiled at the work of the gospel. They persevered against fierce opposition. They carefully guarded the purity of the church. They were vigilant to protect God's people from the constant threat of false teachers. They endured severe persecution and suffering. And they had not grown weary, or succumbed to disappointment and frustration. Through it all, the Lord says the supreme motive for these faithful Ephesians was not some personal agenda or ambition. No, they did it for the sake of His name. The glory of Christ and the testimony of His gospel were always in focus, fixed as the driving force behind the life of the church.

From every angle and perspective, this looked like an exemplary church. On the surface it appeared to be a strong, pure body of faithful believers. But the Lord's eyes are "like a flame of fire."

Nothing escapes His penetrating, omniscient view. And deep below the surface, at its core, the Ephesian church carried a spiritually fatal flaw.

FROM COMMENDATION TO CONDEMNATION

Verse 4 spells out the Ephesians spiritual failure and the cause for Christ's rebuke: "But I have this against you, that you have left your first love." The burning hearts they once had for Christ in the days after they were delivered from the kingdom of darkness had flickered and faded over time. Four decades had passed between the early days of the church under Paul and John's vision on Patmos. The passion of that first generation had cooled, and the second generation simply followed the pattern handed down to them. Their collective devotion to Christ was being replaced by dutiful coldness. While they maintained all the right external behaviors and held to doctrinal orthodoxy, their service to the Lord was no longer prompted by their original fiery love for Him. It was tending toward rote behavior—mechanical piety.

More than once, the Lord rebuked Israel for the same failure. His condemning words to His people illustrate for us the grave danger of allowing love for the Lord to cool and fade. The Lord commanded the prophet Jeremiah,

> "Go and proclaim in the ears of Jerusalem, saying, 'Thus says the LORD,
>
> > "I remember concerning you the devotion of your youth,
> > The love of your betrothals,
> > Your following after Me in the wilderness,
> > Through a land not sown.
> > "Israel was holy to the LORD,
> > The first of His harvest.

All who ate of it became guilty;
Evil came upon them," declares the LORD.'"

Hear the word of the LORD, O house of Jacob, and all
the families of the house of Israel. Thus says the LORD,

"What injustice did your fathers find in Me,
That they went far from Me
And walked after emptiness and became empty?
"They did not say, 'Where is the LORD
Who brought us up out of the land of Egypt,
Who led us through the wilderness,
Through a land of deserts and of pits,
Through a land of drought and of deep darkness,
Through a land that no one crossed
And where no man dwelt?'
"I brought you into the fruitful land
To eat its fruit and its good things.
But you came and defiled My land,
And My inheritance you made an abomination.
"The priests did not say, 'Where is the LORD?'
And those who handle the law did not know Me;
The rulers also transgressed against Me,
And the prophets prophesied by Baal
And walked after things that did not profit.

"Therefore I will yet contend with you," declares the LORD,
"And with your sons' sons I will contend.
"For cross to the coastlands of Kittim and see,
And send to Kedar and observe closely
And see if there has been such a thing as this!
"Has a nation changed gods
When they were not gods?

But My people have changed their glory
For that which does not profit.
"Be appalled, O heavens, at this,
And shudder, be very desolate," declares the LORD.
"For My people have committed two evils:
They have forsaken Me,
The fountain of living waters,
To hew for themselves cisterns,
Broken cisterns
That can hold no water.
(JER. 2:2–13)

In a striking passage that should help believers understand the severity of abandoning their first love, the Lord, through Ezekiel, condemns Israel for forsaking her relationship with Him.

"Then I passed by you and saw you, and behold, you were at the time for love; so I spread My skirt over you and covered your nakedness. I also swore to you and entered into a covenant with you so that you became Mine," declares the Lord GOD. "Then I bathed you with water, washed off your blood from you and anointed you with oil. I also clothed you with embroidered cloth and put sandals of porpoise skin on your feet; and I wrapped you with fine linen and covered you with silk. I adorned you with ornaments, put bracelets on your hands and a necklace around your neck. I also put a ring in your nostril, earrings in your ears and a beautiful crown on your head. Thus you were adorned with gold and silver, and your dress was of fine linen, silk and embroidered cloth. You ate fine flour, honey and oil; so you were exceedingly beautiful and advanced to royalty. Then your fame went forth among the nations on account of your beauty, for it

was perfect because of My splendor which I bestowed on
you," declares the Lord God.

"But you trusted in your beauty and played the harlot
because of your fame, and you poured out your harlotries
on every passer-by who might be willing."
(EZEK. 16:8–15)

In that sense, even Christ's commendation for the Ephesian
church becomes part of its condemnation. He says, in effect, "Yes,
you are doctrinally and morally pure. You're zealous, hardwork-
ing, and disciplined. You were born in the heart of paganism, and
authenticated by miraculous signs and wonders. You were built up
through an explosion of the gospel. You've had the best possible
leadership, and you enjoy their rich heritage to this day. You had it
all. And you still come faithfully. You still work, you still give, and
you still believe. You still worship, and you still hold to the truth.
But I know you don't love Me like you did."

The message is clear: "Turn back. Do not abandon Me."

This is a danger for every believer, and every church—particularly
those like Ephesus, that can easily slip into loveless patterns of piety
and service. Just as we need to toil at the work of God's kingdom,
we need to work to fan the flames of our love for His Son. We must
not be satisfied with cold-hearted, robotic service rendered unto
Him. We cannot allow our hearts to cool toward our Savior. The
cost is far too high.

Consider the chain reaction of forsaking your first love. Fading
love for Christ is the forerunner of spiritual apathy. Apathy is the
forerunner to loving something else. And love for something else
means competing priorities with Christ, which in turn leads to
compromise with the world and corruption, resulting ultimately in
judgment. We will see that pattern play out repeatedly in Christ's
letters to the other churches as He calls on them to repent.

But Ephesus was still on the precipice. Though they had forsaken their first love and drifted into spiritual apathy, they had not yet surrendered their collective heart to something else. Nor had they compromised with the world and fallen into corruption. There was still time to repent and return to the love that once marked their relationship with the Lord.

THE CALL TO ACTION

Christ commands them to do just that. "Therefore remember from where you have fallen, and repent and do the deeds you did at first; or else I am coming to you and will remove your lampstand out of its place—unless you repent" (Rev. 2:5). This is the Great Physician's prescription to restore their flagging affection.

The first step in rekindling love for the Lord is to "remember from where you have fallen." Think back to the first days of your new life in Christ. Remember the glorious heights of your new-found freedom from sin. Remember the joy of the Lord and the gratefulness of your redeemed heart. Remember your love for God's people and your insatiable hunger for His Word. Remember the Spirit's illuminating work, and the transformation of your heart, will, and mind. Remember the unprecedented comfort of true, biblical assurance. We ought to think of these things frequently to stoke the flames of our love for Christ.

But the Lord is not satisfied with mere wistful sentiment as if it were first love. We must also "repent and do the deeds you did at first." That's how you restore a loving relationship—you go back and do what you did at the beginning. Break the cycle of cold, mechanical service to the Lord, and reestablish the habits of loving devotion. There is no better way to demonstrate genuine repentance than to return to the patterns you have forsaken. For the Ephesians, that meant rediscovering the richness of their devotion to God, His Word, and the work of His kingdom.

I hope you find great comfort in the fact that they were called to repent at all. No Christian is able to maintain his or her love for Christ easily. Sin always encroaches and diminishes our devotion to Him, even if only momentarily and periodically. But considering the great heights that the Ephesians had fallen from, it's a powerful encouragement to know that the fall is not permanent, that our love can be renewed and our relationship restored. There is fullness of grace even in God's judgment, and rich mercy in His call to repent.

And if the congregation didn't heed Christ's warning and return to their first love, then what? The Lord answered, "I am coming to you and will remove your lampstand out of its place—unless you repent." The Lord would not tolerate a church with diminishing love for Him. If the Ephesians did not repent, the Lord would snuff out their lampstand. Put simply, it would mean the end of that church.

History does not tell us how the church at Ephesus initially responded to Christ's call for repentance. Perhaps there was a period of rekindling their first love. Perhaps they heeded the threat of Christ's judgment on them. But eventually, the Lord did remove their lampstand. There is no church in Ephesus today—there's not even a city there. If that church could be brought down from such great spiritual heights, should we expect any different action from the Lord on churches today succumbing to the same failures? We need to remember Solomon's wise counsel: "Watch over your heart with all diligence, for from it flow the springs of life" (Prov. 4:23). We must guard our hearts and cherish our first love for Christ.

Hosea was one of the many prophets tasked with calling a back-slidden Israel to repent after their love for God had cooled and faded. He closed his plea to that wayward nation with words of comfort and a promise:

> Return, O Israel, to the LORD your God,
> For you have stumbled because of your iniquity.
> Take words with you and return to the LORD.

Say to Him, "Take away all iniquity
And receive us graciously,
That we may present the fruit of our lips.
"Assyria will not save us,
We will not ride on horses;
Nor will we say again, 'Our god,'
To the work of our hands;
For in You the orphan finds mercy."
(HOS. 14:1–3)

In response to such repentance, the Lord promises, "I will heal their apostasy, I will love them freely" (v. 4).

In Revelation 2, Christ likewise ends His letter to Ephesus with an exhortation and a promise: "He who has an ear, let him hear what the Spirit says to the churches. To him who overcomes, I will grant to eat of the tree of life which is in the Paradise of God" (Rev. 2:7). This is not a closing remark for the Ephesians alone; it's a word of counsel to everyone who reads these letters. The phrase "he who has an ear, let him hear what the Spirit says to the churches" is repeated in all of Christ's seven letters. The implication is that these letters were never intended to have a single audience or a short shelf life. They stand as warnings to all believers and all churches everywhere, throughout all of church history. This was not just a warning to Ephesus; the whole church needs to feel the weight of these words. The Word of God through Peter strengthens this message: "Judgment must begin at the house of God" (1 Peter 4:17 KJV).

For those who will hear, there is a promise attached: "to him who overcomes." Similar phrasing appears in every letter, always emphasizing a blessing for the "overcomers." This is not a call to attain some higher spiritual life. It's simply a way to identify true Christians. John's first epistle shows us what Christ is referring to here: "For whatever is born of God overcomes the world; and this is the victory that has overcome the world—our faith. Who is the one who overcomes the world, but he who believes that Jesus is the Son of God?" (1 John 5:4–5). All believers are "overcomers"—their faith in the Lord Jesus has lifted them out of the dark world into the light of God's kingdom.

And the Lord promises a rich blessing to His overcomers: they will "eat of the tree of life which is in the Paradise of God" (Rev. 2:7). The "tree of life" first appeared in the garden of Eden, along with the tree of the knowledge of good and evil (Gen. 2:9). After Adam and Eve were corrupted by sin, they were banished from the garden to cut off their access to the tree of life (3:22–24). They were under the sentence of death. In Revelation 22, the tree of life appears again (vv. 2, 14, 19)—this time, it symbolizes eternal life with God in heaven.

Christ's promise to the overcomers is clear and direct: *If you believe in Me, you will be rescued from this perishing world and given a home with Me for eternity.* While sin in the church invites the Lord's judgment against His people, it does not mitigate their salvation. This is a promise of the believer's eternal security—that despite our repeated failures to live up to God's holy standard, we are "overcomers" who will not lose our salvation, and that our Lord will hold us fast and deliver us into the Paradise of God for eternity (see John 6:37, 39).

Consider what it might have been like to hear this letter read for the first time in the church at Ephesus. Imagine the horror of knowing the Lord Himself was threatening to shut down your church and drive it out of existence if you didn't repent and return to your first love for Him. You'd be panic-stricken. So Christ closes with this comforting eternal promise for His redeemed church. *You need to repent when your love fades; temporal judgment is coming if you don't. But your future is still safe with Me.* Just as we must heed Christ's words of warning to His churches, we need to rest in the security of our salvation, knowing that nothing—not even our own sinful failures—can separate us from the love of God (Rom. 8:38–39).

4

The Persecuted Church

SMYRNA

Through the years, I've had the privilege of traveling through Eastern Europe and the former Soviet Union. On those trips, I met with many pastors who had suffered severe persecution in communist Russia. They told me what it had been like—how they couldn't get an education or keep a job. They lived under constant surveillance and abuse by the authorities. Some were banished to Siberia, and I heard of many more who had died for their faith. Most churches were forced to meet in secret, always knowing that discovery could mean imprisonment, torture, and even death. That was life under the aggressive atheism of communism. And we know Christians today live under similar circumstances in parts of the world still dominated by communism or Islam.

However, after the Iron Curtain fell, what amazed me was the remarkable strength of those persecuted churches. Everywhere I went, I met devout, dedicated Christians. The years of persecution had forged them into a pure church, zealous for the truth and deeply devoted to Christ. Their faith was alive and genuine, unleashed after years of suffering through fierce opposition.

The believers in Smyrna were similarly purified by persecution, and praised by the Lord of the church for their steadfast faithfulness. Theirs was the kind of Christian character that is born out of hardship and opposition.

THE FRUIT OF PERSECUTION

When the Lord told His disciples "I will build My church" in Matthew 16:18, He included the promise that "the gates of Hades will not overpower it." The "gates of Hades" was a common euphemism for death. What He was saying is that Satan was going to attack the church with deadly force. And as church history reveals to us, Satan has continuously waged a relentless, hell-bent assault on the church. The entire world system hates God, His Word, and His true church.

As a result, Christians should expect to face persecution. In 2 Timothy 3:12, Paul said, "All who desire to live godly in Christ Jesus will be persecuted." Peter told his readers, "Beloved, do not be surprised at the fiery ordeal among you, which comes upon you for your testing, as though some strange thing were happening to you" (1 Peter 4:12). Suffering is not out of the ordinary; but neither is it without purpose. "After you have suffered for a little while, the God of all grace, who called you to His eternal glory in Christ, will Himself perfect, confirm, strengthen and establish you" (1 Peter 5:10). That is the divine comfort for believers—that we do not toil and suffer in this world in vain. James tells us to greet trials and suffering with *joy*, "knowing that the testing of your faith produces endurance. And let endurance have its perfect result, so that you may be perfect and complete, lacking in nothing" (James 1:3–4). Consider this: for Christians, there is no such thing as meaningless suffering. The Lord is always refining us, always sharpening us for the building of His church.

There are also the purifying effects to consider. Hypocrites and charlatans don't stand up in the face of persecution; they run. Heretics and hirelings don't last long when the church is under fire. And those who make merchandise of the faith are forced to close up shop when the very name of God is outlawed. Persecution purges the church of false teachers, false gospels, and false professions of faith. If the church today is on the cusp of another wave of persecution—as it seems—it will be beneficial. As Peter said, even the fiercest persecution comes to us with great spiritual benefits. It perfects and confirms our faith, it strengthens our commitment to the Lord, and it establishes His church in the world aligned against it. Persecution doesn't destroy the church; it makes it strong.

Paul declared that reality out of his own experience:

> And He has said to me, "My grace is sufficient for you, for power is perfected in weakness." Most gladly, therefore, I will rather boast about my weaknesses, so that the power of Christ may dwell in me. Therefore I am well content with weaknesses, with insults, with distresses, with persecutions, with difficulties, for Christ's sake; for when I am weak, then I am strong.
> (2 COR. 12:9–10)

Such was the case in Smyrna.

THE CITY AND THE CHURCH

Located on the coast of the Aegean Sea almost forty miles north of Ephesus, Smyrna was, historians tell us, the most beautiful city in Asia Minor. From the bay, the city stretched up into rolling foothills and the Pagos, a hill that was home to temples in honor of several gods and goddesses, including Zeus, Apollo, Aphrodite, Asclepius, and Cybele. To cover all the religious bases, they had temples for Caesar and Rome as well. Smyrna was also known for science, medicine, and academics. Homer was supposedly born in Smyrna (there was a temple for him, too). It was also one of the oldest cities in the region, possibly first settled as early as 3,000 BC. The Smyrna of the apostle John's day had been rebuilt in 290 BC by successors of Alexander the Great. Unlike Ephesus, Smyrna is still a thriving city to this day. It's now known as Izmir, one of the largest cities in Turkey.

And in Smyrna, there are still Christians. While most of the churches are Catholic, Coptic, Orthodox, or Syriac, there are indications that faithful, Bible-believing Christians still live in Izmir to this day, under fierce persecution at the hands of Muslims. The Lord eventually removed the lampstand from Ephesus, but there is still light in Smyrna.

We don't know when the gospel first reached the city. The church was likely founded during Paul's ministry in Ephesus, when "all who lived in Asia heard the word of the Lord" (Acts 19:10). Acts doesn't give us any insight into the life of the church at Smyrna. The few biblical details we know about this faithful congregation come from Christ's own words to them in Revelation.

As the Lord does in each of His letters to the seven churches, He begins by vividly identifying Himself as the letter's author. To the church at Smyrna, He refers to Himself as "the first and the last, who was dead, and has come to life" (Rev. 2:8). This is an echo of the Lord's comforting words in John's initial vision: "Do not be afraid; I am the first and the last, and the living One; and I was dead, and behold, I am alive forevermore, and have the keys of death and of Hades" (1:17–18).

"The first and the last" was an Old Testament title for God (see Isa. 44:6; 48:12). It's an affirmation of Christ's divine nature and authority. Christ asserts that title again at the end of Revelation, proclaiming, "I am the Alpha and Omega, the first and the last, the beginning and the end" (Rev. 22:13). Our God is eternal. He was already in existence when all things were created, and He will remain after the destruction of all things. He transcends time, space, and all of creation.

And yet, for the sake of wretched sinners, He "was dead, and has come to life." How does an infinite God die? Only in the incarnation of Jesus Christ, as He took on human flesh to die a substitutionary death on our behalf. Peter tells us Christ was "put to death in the flesh, but made alive in the spirit" (1 Peter 3:18). He died as a man for sin and now lives, as the author of Hebrews puts it, "according to the power of an indestructible life" (Heb. 7:16). Death could not hold Him. The body of Jesus died and went into the grave. But "Christ . . . was neither abandoned to Hades, nor did His flesh suffer decay" (Acts 2:31). His resurrection from the dead is the proof that God accepted His sacrifice as full atonement for sin. The resurrection is also the guarantee of our hope for an eternity with Him.

Those would have been particularly comforting words to the beleaguered church of Smyrna. Despised, pursued, oppressed, and outnumbered, there could be no greater encouragement than to hear from the Lord Himself, who suffered far worse than they had been chosen to endure (see Heb. 12:3–4). With the Lord by their side, they could face any threat—even death itself. They could cling to Christ's promise in John's gospel, "I am the resurrection and the life; he who believes in Me will live even if he dies, and everyone who lives and believes in Me will never die" (John 11:25–26). Death could not hold them any more than it could hold Him.

In Revelation 2:9, the Lord continues His reassuring words: "I know your tribulation and your poverty (but you are rich), and the blasphemy by those who say they are Jews and are not, but are a synagogue of Satan."

Needless to say, Smyrna was a difficult place to be a Christian. The believers there likely faced persecution on multiple fronts. To begin with, the city was deeply devoted to the worship of Caesar and the celebration of all things Rome. They even worshiped Rome itself—the *Dea Roma* was a goddess who personified the city. During Domitian's reign, annual sacrifices to Caesar were mandatory; refusing to offer them was a capital offense. In fact, simply failing to say the words "Caesar is Lord" when prompted could cost a believer his life. While Christians could submit to Rome's civil authority (see Rom. 13:1–7), they could not partake in the idolatrous devotion to Caesar. Maintaining that dividing line made them look like seditious rebels, incurring Rome's wrath.

In addition, Smyrna was awash in paganism. They fastidiously worshiped all the gods housed on the Pagos, and many more. Pagan temples, festivals, and rituals of every kind dominated the social life of the city. And believers avoided it all. Christians in Smyrna were out of sync with the culture in every way. Moreover, they worshiped an invisible God—a completely counterintuitive idea in the ancient world, which led to false accusations of atheism.

Adding to those forms of persecution was their "poverty" (Rev. 2:9). The believers in Smyrna weren't just poor. The Greek word here (*ptocheia*) means they had nothing. They lacked not only basic resources, but also the means to improve their situation. It's possible that many in the church were slaves. And whatever meager possessions they may have once owned were likely forfeited in the persecution of believers. They were destitute, barely surviving on whatever they could scrounge together.

However, Christ includes a curious parenthetical note: "I know . . . your poverty (but you are rich)." Contrast that with His condemning words to the church at Laodicea: "You say, 'I am rich, and have become wealthy, and have need of nothing,' and you do not know that you are wretched and miserable and poor and blind and naked" (3:17). The Laodiceans might have had material wealth, but in the things that mattered most—faithfulness, holiness, perseverance, and love for God—they were spiritually bankrupt. Conversely, the Christians in Smyrna had nothing, but they were spiritually rich.

THE SYNAGOGUE OF SATAN

There was one other major front of persecution for the tormented believers in Smyrna. Christ describes it in Revelation 2:9 as "the blasphemy by those who say they are Jews and are not, but are a synagogue of Satan." The Jewish community in Smyrna hated the Christians. They spread vicious gossip about the church, poisoning the minds of the people and inciting the local government. Why? Because they fiercely despised the gospel of Jesus Christ and anyone who declared Him to be the long-awaited Messiah.

Israel's religious leaders endlessly schemed to stifle the progress of the gospel and silence the apostles. Luke recorded many of their attempts in the book of Acts. In Acts 4:18, for example, the Sanhedrin commanded the apostles "not to speak or teach at all in the name of Jesus." When the apostles continued, "the high priest rose up, along with all his associates (that is the sect of the Sadducees), and they were filled with jealousy. They laid hands on the apostles and put them in a public jail" (5:17–18). Acts 13 records the Jewish leaders' reaction to Paul's preaching in Antioch. "But when the Jews saw the crowds, they were filled with jealousy and began contradicting the things spoken by Paul, and were blaspheming. . . . But the Jews incited the devout women of prominence and the leading men of the city, and instigated a persecution against Paul and Barnabas, and drove them out of their district" (13:45, 50). In Iconium, "the Jews who disbelieved stirred up the minds of the Gentiles and embittered them against the brethren. . . . And when an attempt was made by both the Gentiles and the Jews with their rulers, to mistreat and to stone them, they became aware of it and fled" (14:2, 5–6). Luke tells us the trouble followed Paul and his companions to Lystra, where the "Jews came from Antioch and Iconium, and having won over the crowds, they stoned Paul and dragged him out of the city, supposing him to be dead" (14:19). In Thessalonica, "the Jews, becoming jealous and taking along some wicked men from the market place, formed a mob and set the city in an uproar" (17:5). That was the kind of treacherous persecution the Jews in Smyrna were bringing against the church. They were so desperate to curtail the growth of the church that they partnered with heathens.

Christ refers to them as the "synagogue of Satan." This is a chilling commentary on the apostasy of New Testament Judaism. Whatever lip service they still paid to the One true God was worthless after they rejected His Son as Messiah. Their religion was every bit as opposed to God's truth as the emperor worship and paganism that dominated Smyrna, and their synagogues as spiritually vacant as the temples littering the Pagos.

The identification of these persecutors as "those who say they are Jews and are not" is not intended to say they were merely masquerading as Jews. Instead, it's an echo of Paul's statement in Romans 2:28–29: "For he is not a Jew who is one outwardly, nor is circumcision that which is outward in the flesh. But he is a Jew who is one inwardly; and circumcision is that which is of the heart, by the Spirit, not by the letter; and his praise is not from men, but from God." By birth they were Jews, but spiritually they were blasphemous pagans and enemies of God.

A LEGACY OF PERSECUTION

The letter to the church at Smyrna contains no rebuke or condemnation. The Lord had nothing but praise for this downtrodden church, and their faithfulness stands as a shining example to all churches everywhere.

However, the letter does carry a warning—not of judgment but of more persecution to come. In Revelation 2:10, the Lord encourages them, "Do not fear what you are about to suffer. Behold, the devil is about to cast some of you into prison, so that you will be tested, and you will have tribulation for ten days." There are no records to tell us how these prophecies were fulfilled in the church of Smyrna. We don't know whom the devil inspired to cast them into prison; just that it was a common destination for believers in that city. Nor do we know specifically what occurred during the ten days of tribulation and testing. Some have suggested that the Lord was using figurative language to indicate longer periods of persecution, but there's no indication in the text that the Lord is referring to something other than ten twenty-four-hour days.

What we do know is that persecution of some kind in Smyrna carried on for decades and turned one of the heroes of the early church into one of its most famous martyrs. Polycarp was the bishop or pastor of the church at Smyrna. Tradition tells us he was ordained to preach by the apostle John—a plausible claim, since he was in his eighties when he was burned at the stake in AD 156, only fifty or sixty years after John wrote the book of Revelation. It's possible he faithfully ministered in the churches of Asia Minor alongside the apostle before his exile to Patmos.

The story of Polycarp's martyrdom illustrates how the entire city was aligned against the church and eager to usher in its demise. History tells us Polycarp died during a festival of public games (under Rome, that meant public executions). The Jews and the pagans banded together and clamored for his head.

Polycarp had no selfish interest in running for his life. He had a dream in which he saw the pillow under his head burning, and was convinced that this was a sign he would be burned alive. But in deference to the church, he did leave the city to stay with friends in the countryside. His pursuers were enraged when they couldn't find him. They seized two children and tortured them until one gave up his location.

Tradition tells us that even the soldiers who arrested him and returned him to the city did not want to see him die. They pled with him to curse God and say, "Caesar is Lord," or offer a simple sacrifice to the emperor to save his own life. We're told the faithful pastor responded, "Eighty and six years have I served Him, and He never did me any injury: how then can I blaspheme my King and my Saviour?"[1]

When news of his capture spread throughout the city, the excitement was so great that crowds gathered whatever scraps of wood they could find in shops and baths to build the bonfire. The Jews were so eager to see him killed that they brought more wood than anyone else, violating the Sabbath in the process. But Polycarp was unmoved by the threat of death. He challenged his persecutors: "Thou threatenest me with fire which burneth for an hour, and after a little is extinguished, but art ignorant of the fire of the coming judgment and of eternal punishment, reserved for the ungodly. But why tarriest thou? Bring forth what thou wilt."[2]

Tradition tells us that his executioners did not nail him to the stake, as was customary. Before they could, Polycarp told them, "Leave me as I am; for He that giveth me strength to endure the fire, will also enable me, without your securing me by nails, to remain without moving in the pile."[3] Some accounts include the detail that he seemed so tranquil amid the flames that someone reached in with a sword to hasten his death.

That's what life was like for the church in Smyrna. Every believer in the church had to live daily in the psalmist's bold proclamation: "In God I put my trust, I will not be afraid. What can man do to me?" (Ps. 56:11).

THE PRIZE OF PERSEVERANCE

Christ's letter to the church closes with a similar sentiment, and a promise of the blessing to come: "Be faithful until death, and I will give you the crown of life" (Rev. 2:10). Don't read that as an ultimatum. The Lord was not giving them yet another hurdle to clear on top of everything else they had already endured. Rather, it's simply an encouragement to keep doing what they had already faithfully been doing, and to bear up under the fierce opposition aligned against them.

In themselves, believers don't have the capacity to maintain or protect their faith. If we could lose our salvation, we certainly would. Instead, it's the Lord who holds us steadfast in faith. Christ repeatedly declared this glorious truth to His disciples. "I give eternal life to them, and they will never perish; and no one will snatch them out of My hand. My Father, who has given them to Me, is greater than all; and no one is able to snatch them out of the Father's hand" (John 10:28–29). "This is the will of Him who sent Me, that of all that He has given Me I lose nothing, but raise it up on the last day" (John 6:39).

In his epistle to the Romans, Paul dismisses any concerns about the security of our salvation:

> And we know that God causes all things to work
> together for good to those who love God, to those who
> are called according to His purpose. For those whom He
> foreknew, He also predestined to become conformed to
> the image of His Son, so that He would be the firstborn
> among many brethren; and these whom He predestined,
> He also called; and these whom He called, He also
> justified; and these whom He justified, He also glorified.
> What then shall we say to these things? If God is for us,
> who is against us?
> (ROM. 8:28–31)

Scripture is clear: If you are a believer, you *will* persevere in the faith. Not because of any inherent strength in you. You have no such strength in yourself. But God Himself "is able to keep you from stumbling, and to make you stand in the presence of His glory blameless with great joy" (Jude 24). And He *does* hold His people fast. "The Lord will rescue me from every evil deed, and will bring me safely to His heavenly kingdom; to Him be the glory forever and ever. Amen" (2 Tim. 4:18). That means if you are truly a believer, your faith will endure to the end. True faith is proven in the fires of persecution. It survives triumphantly.

What does that mean for people who reject Christ and walk away from the faith? John answered that question in his first epistle: "They went out from us, but they were not really of us; for if they had been of us, they would have remained with us; but they went out, so that it would be shown that they all are not of us" (1 John 2:19).

In that sense, the Lord is not merely promising the believers in Smyrna a reward *for* their perseverance. Perseverance *is* the reward, as it bears unimpeachable witness to the genuineness of their faith. And those whose faith is validated by a faithful life will enjoy the crown of eternal life with their Lord and Savior.

The letter ends with a comforting note, to the believers in Smyrna and to the wider audience: "He who has an ear, let him hear what the Spirit says to the churches. He who overcomes will not be hurt by the second death" (Rev. 2:11). Persecution can cost believers a lot. It can damage our livelihood. It can rob us of our homes and possessions. It can sever families and destroy relationships. It can cost us our freedom and our health. In some cases, it costs us our lives. There is no guarantee that we are safe from any of that in this life.

But the Lord promises that His overcomers, believers (see 1 John 5:4–5), will not face the second death. We may have to endure physical death, but there is no threat of spiritual death for those who know and love the Lord. Revelation 20:12–14 describes the spiritual death we've been delivered from:

> I saw the dead, great and small, standing before the throne, and the books were opened; and another book was opened, which is the book of life; and the dead were judged from the things which were written in the books, according to their deeds. And the sea gave up the dead

which were in it, and death and Hades gave up the dead which were in them; and they were judged, every one of them according to their deeds. Then death and Hades were thrown into the lake of fire. This is the second death, the lake of fire.

If you truly love the Lord—if your faith is verified by a life of faithful perseverance—you'll never experience that. If you are a true believer with a faith that overcomes all the persecution Satan can hurl at you, even to the first death, you will never experience the second death. Instead, Christ says to you, "Behold, I am coming quickly, and My reward is with Me, to render to every man according to what he has done. I am the Alpha and the Omega, the first and the last, the beginning and the end. Blessed are those who wash their robes, so that they may have the right to the tree of life, and may enter by the gates into the city" (Rev. 22:12–14).

In the face of suffering and opposition, we need to remember the limits of Satan's persecuting power and the glorious, eternal rewards that await those who persevere.

It's worth noting that *smyrna* is the Greek word used in the Septuagint for myrrh, a strong fragrance used by the Jews to mask the scent of dead bodies. John 19:39–40 tells us that Nicodemus brought roughly a hundred pounds of myrrh mixed with aloes to wrap Christ's body for burial. But myrrh was precious and hard to come by. It was made from the resin of small, thorny trees. Only when it was thoroughly crushed would it yield its pleasing fragrance. In that sense, the church at Smyrna was aptly named. God permitted Satan to crush these believers under constant persecution, and Christ's letter to them confirms the heavenly aroma of their faithfulness.

5

The Compromising Church
PERGAMUM

When God delivered the Israelites from Egypt, He did not merely release them from slavery under Pharaoh; He rescued them from the corrupting influences of Egypt's paganism. Egyptians worshiped a virtually infinite collection of deities. And for centuries, the Israelites lived in close proximity to the madness of Egypt's idolatry, intimately familiar with all their pagan rituals.

Over time, Israel's concept of worship was clouded and distorted. Although they declared their allegiance to God by obeying His commands for the first Passover (Exod. 12:1–13), they were influenced by polytheistic paganism. Even after their miraculous delivery from Egypt through the Red Sea on dry land—on top of all the other miracles the Lord performed before their departure—the hearts and minds of Israel were still caught in the snare of idolatry. That's why when Moses did not immediately return from Mount Sinai, Aaron and the Israelites panicked and fashioned a golden calf to serve as their new god (Exod. 32:1–4). Such is the staggering irrationality of idol worship.

To establish His Law and His pattern for acceptable worship, and to break the chains of paganism's lingering influence among His people, God gave Israel the book of Leviticus. Over and over, it stresses the need for personal holiness and pure worship. It addresses how to deal with sin, how to make appropriate sacrifices, and how to protect the purity of God's people. Leviticus 18:1–5 is the heart of the book. In these verses, God delivers His fundamental commands to reject the practices of the surrounding pagan nations:

> Then the LORD spoke to Moses, saying, "Speak to the
> sons of Israel and say to them, 'I am the LORD your God.
> You shall not do what is done in the land of Egypt where
> you lived, nor are you to do what is done in the land of
> Canaan where I am bringing you; you shall not walk in
> their statutes. You are to perform My judgments and
> keep My statutes, to live in accord with them; I am the
> LORD your God. So you shall keep My statutes and My
> judgments, by which a man may live if he does them; I
> am the LORD.'"

This is God laying claim to His own. He's basically saying, "You are no longer idolaters. You are now the people of the true and living God. You cannot continue after the pattern of the pagan nations. You will worship Me alone." The subsequent verses spell out specific prohibitions against the immorality that constituted much of pagan worship. It's a shocking list of deviant behaviors: adultery, homosexuality, incest, bestiality, and child sacrifice. Those vile perversions were everyday activities in Egypt, Canaan, and every other culture dominated by paganism.

The Lord then reiterates His earlier commandment, "Do not defile yourselves by any of these things; for by all these the nations which I am casting out before you have become defiled. . . . Thus you are to keep My charge, that you do not practice any of the abominable customs which have been practiced before you, so as not to defile yourselves with them; I am the LORD your God" (vv. 24, 30). His exhortation continues into chapter 19: "Speak to all the congregation of the sons of Israel and say to them, 'You shall be holy, for I the LORD your God am holy. . . . Do not turn to idols or make for yourselves molten gods; I am the LORD your God'" (vv. 1–2, 4).

This is a call for spiritual separation; to be wholly distinct and divided from the wickedness of the world's system. The Lord demands pure worship. He demands single-minded devotion. God commanded Israel to be separated from the corrupting influences of the world.

And He desires the same separation for His church.

THE SINNER-FRIENDLY CHURCH

The term *worldliness* sounds archaic to many in the church today. They dismiss it as a concern for a gentler, less-enlightened time, back when card games and dancing were considered major threats to the sanctity and purity of the church. In fact, some believers are so enamored with their freedom in Christ that they view any discussion of worldliness as a worn-out legalistic imposition. In spite of the clear statement from heaven that "friendship with the world is hostility [hatred] toward God" and that "whoever wishes to be a friend of the world makes himself an enemy of God" (James 4:4), the suggestion that Christians should separate themselves from worldly values and worldly amusements is a nonstarter.

Instead, the church today works incredibly hard to appear as much like the culture as possible. For decades, it has been popular for church leaders to make their services look, sound, and feel exactly like secular gatherings and events. Many churches today are indistinguishable from the concert venues and theaters of the world. They fastidiously imitate the latest styles in fashion and pop-culture trends, desperate to seem relevant and cool.

Such events are built on a philosophy of pragmatism: if it produces the desired effect, they'll do it. The result is a church that is sinner-friendly, not God-friendly, and certainly not sinner-frightening. It's a show built in the image of the pagan world, where popular methodology and strategy dominate Scripture, doctrine, and spiritual power. And as the world grows increasingly hostile to the gospel, the sinner-friendly church must compromise more and more to maintain its attractiveness. Refusing to be an offense to anyone, they emphasize physical emotion, not spiritual worship; affirmation, not conviction; sentimentality, not theology; entertainment, not edification; and frivolity, not solemnity.

Worse still, they're petrified of rejection and persecution, so they will always fall in line with the world's expectations and ever-changing social norms. Many churches today turn a blind eye to sexual immorality; others won't talk about sin *at all*. They ignore the topic, occasionally focusing on troublesome issues in life, but never declaring the power, presence, and destructive damage of sin or naming it as an offense to God's holiness requiring judgment. It's a therapeutic church culture, designed to make sinners feel comfortable, welcome, and validated at any cost.

But worldliness does not make the gospel look attractive; it makes it look impotent. These churches need to realize the grave disservice they are doing to the cause of Christ and the progress of the gospel. A church that's just like the world has nothing to offer to the world—it's merely one more disposable entertainment. And how could they think such worldliness could be offered to God as worship?

Scripture tells us this is not a new phenomenon. Our Lord said,

> "If the world hates you, you know that it has hated Me
> before it hated you. If you were of the world, the world
> would love its own; but because you are not of the world,
> but I chose you out of the world, because of this the

world hates you. Remember the word that I said to you,
'A slave is not greater than his master.' If they persecuted
Me, they will also persecute you; if they kept My word,
they will keep yours also."
(JOHN 15:18–20)

Where the Word of the gospel is faithfully proclaimed, the hatred of the world will follow.

Since the earliest days of the church, believers have caved under pressure to accommodate the world. Christ's letter to the church at Pergamum in Revelation establishes the severe dangers of such compromise.

A CHURCH IN THE CROSSHAIRS

Pergamum was the capital city of Asia Minor, situated about a hundred miles north of Ephesus. It was not a port city. Nor did it sit along any major trade routes. Instead, it was a center for culture, education, and religion. The city's most notable feature was its impressive library. With 200,000 volumes—all handwritten—it was second only to the library in Alexandria. Tradition says that the use of animal skin parchment was developed in Pergamum to keep up with demand for writing material. The vast collection was eventually sent as a gift from Marc Antony to Cleopatra.

Pergamum was situated on a large hill, standing a thousand feet over the plains below. Nineteenth-century archeologist Sir William Ramsey described its authoritative stance: "Beyond all other sites in Asia Minor it gives the traveller the impression of a royal city, the home of authority: the rocky hill on which it stands is so huge, and dominates the broad plain of the Caicus [River valley] so proudly and boldly."[1] You can visit the ruins of Pergamum today near the Turkish city of Bergama.

Scripture doesn't tell us when the church in Pergamum was

founded. It could have been during Paul's second missionary journey, when he passed through the nearby region of Mysia (Acts 16:7–8). More likely, it was founded during his ministry in Ephesus, as the gospel spread rapidly from that church throughout Asia Minor (Acts 19:10).

In the apostle John's day, Pergamum saw itself as a defender of Greek culture in Asia Minor. There were temples dedicated to Zeus, Athena, Asklepios, and Dionysos. However, the city was dominated by emperor worship. In honor of Emperor Augustus, Pergamum built the first temple devoted to the cultic religion in 29 BC. Two more would follow, to Trajan and Septimus Severus. Pergamum held a fervent religious devotion to Rome and its emperor. In neighboring cities, Christians faced danger and persecution annually if they failed to make the yearly sacrifice to Caesar. It was a daily threat in Pergamum.

While the church in Pergamum was in great danger from the world, it was in even greater danger from the Lord. Unlike the letters to Ephesus and Smyrna, Christ's letter to Pergamum starts with a threat. The Lord identifies Himself as "the One who has the two-edged sword" (Rev. 2:12). This is not a comforting salutation. It's an immediate warning, meant to evoke the same terror it inspired in the apostle John in his initial vision (1:17). Christ is coming in judgment, wielding His Word like a mighty broadsword—a sword that has no dull edges (see Heb. 4:12). Later in Revelation, John tells us this is how the unrepentant world will see Christ when He comes in His final judgment: "From His mouth comes a sharp sword, so that with it He may strike down the nations, and He will rule them with a rod of iron; and He treads the wine press of the fierce wrath of God, the Almighty" (19:15). That is the same Lord who is writing to the church at Pergamum.

However, He includes a note of commendation. Although the Pergamum church was guilty of compromise with the world, it was not bereft of faithful believers. The Lord says, "I know where you dwell, where Satan's throne is; and you hold fast My name, and did not deny My faith even in the days of Antipas, My witness, My faithful one, who was killed among you, where Satan dwells" (2:13).

Historians and commentators offer some suggestions regarding what the Lord was referring to as "Satan's throne." Pergamum was home to a massive altar to Zeus, the god of war. The huge structure dominated the city's acropolis. Describing its massive scale, Edwin Yamauchi writes, "The word *altar* is somewhat misleading. The structure is a monumental colonnaded court in the form of a horseshoe, 120 by 112 feet. The podium of the altar was nearly 18 feet high. The great frieze, which ran at the base of the structure for 446 feet, depicted a gigantomachy, that is, a battle of the gods and the giants. It was one of the greatest works of Hellenistic art."[2] Certainly, such a grand monument to Zeus—but in reality, dedicated to the devil—could have served as Satan's throne.

Others believe it is a reference to the shrine of Asclepius, the Greek god of healing, who was depicted as a snake. The temple in his honor was overrun with nonpoisonous snakes that supposedly imparted his healing power. Pilgrims would travel from all over the region to worship in the temple, which involved lying or sleeping on the ground among the snakes. Since Satan is repeatedly depicted as a serpent in John's visions (Rev. 12:9, 14, 15; 20:2), this could have been an early instance of that imagery.

It could also be a reference to the dominating cult of emperor worship, which was the most powerful religious influence in the city and posed the greatest opposition to believers. Simply declining to repeat the phrase "Caesar is Lord" could lead to death. The exclusivity of the gospel made Christians a target for Rome's most fastidious supplicants. "Satan's throne" may simply be referring to the true power behind the cult of Caesar.

Any or all of those features of Pergamum's paganism could justify the reference to Satan's throne. And the multitude of potential locations lends further credence to Christ's claim that Pergamum was the city "where Satan dwells." In that sense, it could also be a general reference to Satan's preeminence throughout the city in its various strains of pagan idolatry. The inhabitants of Pergamum thought they observed a diverse collection of gods and goddesses. We know they were only worshiping the devil. As the apostle Paul wrote, "The things which the Gentiles sacrifice [to idols], they sacrifice to demons and not to God" (1 Cor. 10:20).

In spite of the Satanic religion that dominated the city, the Lord notes that the believers in Pergamum "hold fast My name, and did not deny My faith even in the days of Antipas, My witness, My faithful one, who was killed among you." They clung to the Savior. Like John, who was exiled "because of the word of God and the testimony of Jesus" (Rev. 1:9), the church never wavered in their commitment to Christ. They refused to deny the faith.

But that steadfast commitment to the gospel was costly in the ancient pagan world. The "days of Antipas" likely referred to a period of fierce persecution for the church. Scripture doesn't tell us anything else about Antipas, but his name was instantly familiar to the believers in Pergamum. The word translated "witness" (*martus*) became synonymous with believers whose witness for Christ cost them their lives, giving us the transliterated English word *martyr*. Tradition holds that Antipas was a leader in the church, and that he was roasted to death inside a brass bull during Domitian's campaign of persecution. Regardless of how Antipas was murdered, Christ singles out and commends his exemplary faithfulness unto death.

It's worth noting the possessive pronoun the Lord employs throughout Revelation 2:13: "You hold fast *My* name, and did not deny *My* faith even in the days of Antipas, *My* witness, *My* faithful one" (emphasis added). Christ has a claim on this church; it belongs to Him. And that further emphasizes what an egregious sin their compromise was.

FRIENDSHIP WITH THE WORLD

After that brief word of praise, the letter pivots back to judgment: "But I have a few things against you, because you have there some who hold to the teaching of Balaam, who kept teaching Balak to put a stumbling block before the sons of Israel, to eat things sacrificed to idols and to commit acts of immorality. So you also have some who in the same way hold the teaching of the Nicolaitans" (Rev. 2:14–15).

In spite of the church's faithfulness to the gospel, some were engaging in idolatry. Remember that in the ancient world, there was no distinction between the sacred and the secular. Religion was not an isolated part of life; it set the course for the culture. Virtually all aspects of society were intertwined with temple rituals, festivals, and celebrations. Just like post-Exodus Israel falling back into idolatry, some in the church at Pergamum were venturing back to the habits of paganism. And they were encouraging others in the church to do the same.

How do we know that? The Lord singles out those "who hold to the teaching of Balaam, who kept teaching Balak to put a stumbling block before the sons of Israel" (v. 14). This is a reference to Numbers 22-25 and Israel's conflict with Moab. Balak was the king of Moab. He had heard of Israel's miraculous deliverance from Egypt. Scripture tells us he "saw all that Israel had done to the Amorites. . . . and Moab was in dread of the sons of Israel" (Num. 22:2–3). Balak knew about the God of the Israelites, and he was terrified of what his new neighbors could potentially do to him and his nation.

So Balak sent for Balaam, a notorious prophet-for-hire and supposed sorcerer, to put a curse on Israel for him. Balaam made three attempts to curse Israel, but the Lord stifled him each time, instead using his mouth to bless Israel. So Balaam developed another strategy: if he couldn't curse Israel, he would *corrupt* them. Numbers 25:1–2 says, "While Israel remained at Shittim, the people began to play the harlot with the daughters of Moab. For they invited the people to the sacrifices of their gods, and the people ate and bowed down to their gods" (see also 31:16). Balaam persuaded the women of Moab to intermarry with the men of Israel, pulling those men into the idolatrous, immoral culture of Moab. They went back to eating things sacrificed to idols, back to the perverse sexual immorality of idolatry. They were coaxed back into the paganism they had escaped in Egypt, seduced into a blasphemous union with Satan. "So Israel joined themselves to Baal of Peor, and the Lord was angry against Israel" (25:3). This was a severe and widespread spiritual betrayal. The Lord's chastening included the slaughter of 24,000 men of Israel (v. 9).

That was the "teaching of Balaam" that some in the church at Pergamum held to—they were throwing the same seductive stumbling block in front of the believers there. The Lord had delivered these men and women from the vile corruptions of pagan idolatry. Now others in the church were inviting them to slip back into their old, immoral habits. No doubt some in the Pergamum church were falling to these sirens of Satan's culture. Practically speaking, that meant some in the church were attending pagan feasts, taking part in the perverse debauchery, and then coming to church. In his second epistle, Peter delivers a scathing condemnation against those "who indulge the flesh in its corrupt desires" (2 Peter 2:10) and attempt to lure believers back into similar wickedness. Peter writes further,

> They count it a pleasure to revel in the daytime. They are stains and blemishes, reveling in their deceptions, as they carouse with you, having eyes full of adultery that never cease from sin, enticing unstable souls, having a heart trained in greed, accursed children; forsaking the right way, they have gone astray, having followed the way of Balaam, the son of Beor, who loved the wages of unrighteousness. (vv. 13–15)

These corrupters of the faithful took pleasure in their deception as they lured believers back into the bondage of sin.

That wasn't the only corrupting influence in the Pergamum church. The Lord also notes, "You also have some who in the same way hold to the teaching of the Nicolaitans" (Rev. 2:15). As mentioned earlier, we don't know specifically what the Nicolaitans taught. Some of the early church fathers indicated that they lived lives of unchecked indulgence, likely tied to the immorality of paganism. That would make them fitting companions to the Balaamists, and a significant threat to the purity of the believers at Pergamum. Whatever their specific heresies were, we know the Lord hated their deeds (2:6), as well as their presence and influence in the Pergamum church.

And that's really the worst part of it all—that these vile heretics and deceivers were allowed to remain in the church unaddressed and unabated. Christ writes that the Pergamum believers "have there some" (v. 14); "you also have some" (v. 15). While the church held fast to Christ's name and did not deny the faith, they were doing an abysmal job of guarding the flock of God. They sat and watched while wolves made off with the sheep.

Put another way, the church at Pergamum was living out the sinful absurdity of Paul's warning to the Corinthians:

> Do not be bound together with unbelievers; for what partnership have righteousness and lawlessness, or what fellowship has light with darkness? Or what harmony has Christ with Belial, or what has a believer in common with an unbeliever? Or what agreement has the temple of God with idols? For we are the temple of the living God; just as God said, "I will dwell in them and walk among them; and I will be their God, and they shall be My people. Therefore, come out from their midst and be separate," says the Lord. "And do not touch what is unclean; and I will welcome you."
> (2 COR. 6:14–17)

Pergamum had failed to separate thoroughly from the unbelieving world; they had settled for compromise. As we saw, they faithfully held the line on doctrine, but not when it came to holiness. They ought to have heeded the exhortation of the apostle James, written to shake careless church members just like these from their apathetic slumber: "You adulteresses, do you not know that friendship with the world is hostility toward God? Therefore whoever wishes to be a friend of the world makes himself an enemy of God" (James 4:4). Pergamum's friendship with the world was costing it dearly, as precious believers drifted back into the habits of their former lives.

This is a serious and increasingly common characteristic of many churches today. Not enough believers live as "aliens and strangers" in this world. As a result, they're unable to "abstain from fleshly lusts which wage war against the soul" (1 Peter 2:11). We need to remember that it is the calling of the church to sever whatever tethers this world and its values still have on our hearts. We need to fight daily to break the habits of our former lives, training ourselves to hate our once-cherished sins. John had already given the church precisely that admonition in his first epistle:

> Do not love the world nor the things in the world. If anyone loves the world, the love of the Father is not in him. For all that is in the world, the lust of the flesh and the lust of the eyes and the boastful pride of life, is not from the Father, but is from the world. The world is passing away, and also its lusts; but the one who does the will of God lives forever.
>
> (1 JOHN 2:15–17)

Too many churches today give no indication that the world is passing away. They're consumed with the culture, ignorant to the corrupting influences they routinely invite into their midst, or unmoved by the threat they represent. Countless churches—

including many of the largest and most influential evangelical megachurches—are enthralled with themed messages based not on Scripture but on various icons of worldly entertainment: popular movies, television series, hit songs, or even the celebrities who have popularized those things. There's even a Wikipedia entry explaining the term *U2charist*, "a communion service, or Eucharist, accompanied by U2 songs in lieu of traditional hymns."[3] One popular church—by most accounts the third largest evangelical church in America, with more than 30,000 members—devotes a month each summer to a series called "At the Movies." The music, message, and campus decorations are all carefully coordinated to feature themes and messages drawn from whatever Hollywood blockbuster they have chosen to highlight.[4] A few years ago, a different—but similarly influential—megachurch famously opened their Easter service with a rendition of AC/DC's rock anthem "Highway to Hell."[5] Examples similar to those abound on YouTube and other forums on the internet where church leaders discuss church-growth methodology.

The medium has indeed become the message. We live in a time exactly like the apostle Paul foretold, when church members "will not endure sound doctrine; but wanting to have their ears tickled, they . . . accumulate for themselves teachers in accordance to their own desires, and . . . turn away their ears from the truth and . . . turn aside to myths" (2 Tim. 4:3–4).

Just like Pergamum, the modern church's easy familiarity with the world has left it open to the compromises that corrupt. And just like Pergamum, it puts the church in the path of judgment by the Lord Himself.

ENMITY WITH GOD

The Lord spells out the remedy to Pergamum's spiritual compromise in no uncertain terms: "Therefore repent; or else I am coming to you quickly, and I will make war against them with the sword of

My mouth" (Rev. 2:16). In essence, He's saying, "Stop the worldly compromise. Stop tolerating the unequal yoke. Purge the church of these ungodly, immoral influences, or I will do it for you." This command applies to the whole church—both the heretical corrupters and all those who tolerated their deviations. They were all guilty of compromise.

The church must not accommodate the sins of professing believers who insist on living as close as possible to the corrupt culture. "A little leaven leavens the whole lump" (1 Cor. 5:6). We must confront such worldliness (a term mostly absent from church vocabulary today).

And we must be willing to risk offending unbelievers for the sake of the church's purity. Of course, we want to reach out to the lost and welcome unbelievers to hear the gospel. We hope earnestly that "God may grant them repentance leading to the knowledge of the truth" (2 Tim. 2:25). But we also know that only occurs when "they come to their senses and escape from the snare of the devil" (v. 26)—not when they've been lulled into a false sense of acceptance by a compromising church. For the sake of their souls, we must be willing to confront them with the truth about sin, its eternal consequences, and their need for a Savior.

Pergamum also ought to be a warning to every church and every Christian who believes that sound doctrine is enough on its own, that God is interested only in what we affirm, not in how we act. That attitude has grown in popularity in recent years. Pergamum is a reminder that *knowing* the truth and *living* the truth are equally important in the eyes of the Lord. "Prove yourselves doers of the word, and not merely hearers who delude themselves" (James 1:22).

Finally, we must remember the words of Leviticus 18: "I am the LORD your God. You shall not do what is done in the land . . . you shall not walk in their statutes. You are to perform My judgments and keep My statutes, to live in accord with them; I am the LORD your God. So you shall keep My statutes and My judgments, by which a man may live if he does them; I am the LORD" (vv. 2–5).

God's design for His redeemed people is complete separation from everything that characterizes the world. We don't do what they do. We don't think the way they think. We don't talk the way they talk. We don't share the world's values. And we certainly don't need to borrow from worldly belief systems. "Our citizenship is in heaven" (Phil. 3:20). This world is by definition an alien environment for those whose eternal home is heaven.

A PARTING ENCOURAGEMENT

Again, the Lord closes His letter with a note to the wider audience. Though each of these letters is specifically addressed to one local congregation at the end of the first century, our Lord's message has implications that reach far beyond those seven local churches. All seven of Christ's letters speak to the whole church throughout its entire history. We were meant to learn from these examples, both good and bad. But we're also meant to leave encouraged, with our eyes fixed on the eternal privileges of knowing and loving Christ. To that end, the Lord writes, "He who has an ear, let him hear what the Spirit says to the churches. To him who overcomes, to him I will give some of the hidden manna, and I will give him a white stone, and a new name written on the stone, which no one knows but he who receives it" (Rev. 2:17).

To all faithful believers (see 1 John 5:4–5), Christ promises three things. The first is "the hidden manna." Manna was the bread that God supplied to Israel to feed them during their wandering in the wilderness. And like many elements of Israel's covenant with God, the manna pictured (and pointed to) something greater, something eternal and heavenly. Specifically, the manna was one of the great Old Testament symbols of Christ (John 6:48–51). He is the Bread of Life who provides spiritual sustenance to His people. So when He promises faithful believers that He will give them "some of the hidden manna," this is a promise of the spiritual benefits of knowing and loving Him (Eph. 1:3).

Christ also promises His overcomers "a white stone." In the ancient world, victorious athletes received a trophy in the form of a stone with their names inscribed. Not only did it signify their victory, it served as their admission into the great banquet of victors. In terms of eternity, this is a reminder that God's faithful servant will be welcomed into God's lavish provision and blessings in heaven.

Finally, Christ promises "a new name written on the stone, which no one knows but he who receives it." Whenever I have preached on this passage, someone will invariably ask what I think the secret name is. The whole point is that *"no one* knows." It is no doubt a name of personal affection and honor—a name that marks out God's triumphant overcomers and reflects His love for His adopted children.

6

The Corrupt Church
THYATIRA

One of the earliest mentions of "the church" in the New Testament comes from the lips of Christ in Matthew 18. There His first message to the church is for dealing with sin in the assembly. Like His parting words to the churches in Revelation 2–3, Christ's instructions to His church are wholly concerned with the holiness and spiritual health of the church herself. He did not issue a manifesto instructing His people to engage or redeem secular culture. He didn't present a strategy for assessing and addressing the felt needs of the community, or ending cultural inequity, or lowering the poverty rate. He didn't lay out a plan for maximizing the church's political or moral clout. He didn't stress the need for tolerance, validation, spiritual safe spaces, or any of the other currently-fashionable evangelical talking points. Instead, His concern was for the *purity* of His church. He wanted His people to know how to confront and deal with sin.

> "If your brother sins, go and show him his fault in private; if he listens to you, you have won your brother. But

if he does not listen to you, take one or two more with you, so that by the mouth of two or three witnesses every fact may be confirmed. If he refuses to listen to them, tell it to the church; and if he refuses to listen even to the church, let him be to you as a Gentile and a tax collector."
(MATT. 18:15–17)

This unambiguous command for confronting sin in the church is an entirely counterintuitive idea for the hip, cool, modern church. Many think, *Who am I to tell someone else how to live? Why would we want to expose people's sin or force anyone out of the church? Shouldn't we just love them and let the Spirit do His work?* Incredibly, many churches today *proudly* ignore the sin in their midst in the name of tolerance, unity, and love—proving only that they have no true understanding of what the Bible means when it talks about unity and love. Amazingly, ignoring sin and practicing tolerance has become a staple strategy for church growth. This directly defies the Lord's commands.

The apostle Paul harshly rebuked the Corinthians for that very attitude in 1 Corinthians 5. A man in their midst was openly indulging in an incestuous sin so egregious that even Gentiles in the community were shocked by it. "Someone has his father's wife" (v. 1). Instead of excommunicating the man, they boasted about their tolerance, as if it were a badge of honor to allow such a person to represent their fellowship in the community. Paul told them, "You have become arrogant and have not mourned instead, so that the one who had done this deed would be removed from your midst. . . . Your boasting is not good. Do you not know that a little leaven leavens the whole lump of dough?" (vv. 2, 6). Not only was the testimony of the entire church ruined by the open sin of this man; sin itself increases in the church like leaven. Such wickedness, when tolerated, will spread and poison the whole fellowship. The effects of that principle were already clearly evident in the Corinthian assembly.

The apostle's instructions were straightforward and urgent: He commanded them "not to associate with any so-called brother if he is an immoral person, or covetous, or an idolater, or a reviler, or a drunkard, or a swindler—not even to eat with such a one. . . . Remove the wicked man from among yourselves" (vv. 11, 13).

Though sin spreads like leaven, purity and holiness do not. They must be diligently cultivated and protected. Many in the church today seem to be laboring under the bizarre notion that an "acceptable" amount of sin in the church is an evangelistic strategy. They pretend that the Lord's view of unrighteousness and corruption is as casual as theirs is. Believers must defend the purity of the church above all other concerns, regardless of how doing so might offend observing sinners.

In Ephesians 5:25–27, Paul describes the Lord's love for His church and His abiding concern for her purity. He says Christ "loved the church and gave Himself up for her, so that He might sanctify her, having cleansed her by the washing of water with the word, that He might present to Himself the church in all her glory, having no spot or wrinkle or any such thing; but that she would be holy and blameless." Our priorities for the church need to reflect the Lord's. We need to prize the purity of the church as He does.

Consider the ways that overlooked and ignored sin inhibits the work of God's people. He has called the church to be heaven's representative on earth. The church is the place where God is to be honored and glorified, where righteousness is exalted and holiness pursued. In fact, God's people are called to reflect His holiness as a testimony to the unrepentant world (Matt. 5:16). We can't do that if we're tolerating sin in our midst.

Despite Scripture's clear instructions, many churches that declare sound doctrine fail to declare and protect holiness. Christ's letter to the church at Thyatira illustrates the deadly consequences of failing to guard the purity of God's church.

BUILT FOR DESTRUCTION

Thyatira, the smallest of the cities mentioned in Revelation 2–3, was located approximately forty miles to the southeast of Pergamum, along the main road traveling north and south. Though it sat in a flat river valley that lacked any natural fortifications, it was originally founded as a military garrison on the main road to Pergamum. The plan was that any attackers headed toward Pergamum would be slowed by the soldiers at Thyatira, buying precious time for Pergamum to prepare its own defense. As the capital city of the region, Pergamum would surely be the destination for invading forces; Thyatira was merely a speed bump along the way. Therefore, Thyatira was frequently destroyed and rebuilt throughout its history. In the few instances the city is referenced in ancient literature, it is usually to relay the details of its conquest.

Things changed for Thyatira after it came under Roman control. The relative peace brought by the Roman Empire spared the city from constant attack and destruction. And its location along a major trade route connecting Pergamum with Laodicea and Smyrna turned Thyatira into a boomtown for commercial industry. The city specialized in dyed fabrics—particularly a purple dye developed from a combination of shellfish and root—but it was home to all sorts of ancient tradecrafts. History suggests the city was still ascending in prominence when John saw his vision of Christ on Patmos. Today, it is the Turkish city of Akhisar.

Unlike the other cities of Asia Minor, Thyatira never developed into a religious center. They never had an acropolis. The city's primary deity was Apollo, the Greek god of the sun, though religion was not a major feature of public life. Instead, Thyatira was dominated by trade guilds, similar to modern labor unions. There were guilds for dyers, tanners, bronzesmiths, bakers, and every other trade that operated in the city. Finding a job or owning a business was virtually impossible if you weren't part of a trade guild. And each guild submitted to a patron deity and celebrated the associated feasts and rituals. Of course, these events included food sacrificed to idols and sexual immorality—creating a significant dilemma for any Christian believer who wanted to maintain both his purity and his livelihood. While the city itself was relatively secular, the deviance of religious paganism still managed to infect and pollute the culture.

Scripture doesn't tell us when the church at Thyatira was founded. It could have been during Paul's ministry in Ephesus (Acts 19:10). It also could have blossomed out of his earlier ministry in Philippi. In the book of Acts, Luke tells us, "A woman named Lydia, from the city of Thyatira, a seller of purple fabrics, a worshiper of God, was listening; and the Lord opened her heart to respond to the things spoken by Paul" (Acts 16:14). Lydia and her family were the first believers in Europe and helped establish the Philippian church. It's possible that she or some of her relatives returned to Thyatira and helped establish a gospel outpost there.

No matter how the church in Thyatira began, it's instantly apparent from Christ's letter that they had not remained faithful to the truth, or to His instructions to keep the church pure. In fact, the congregation was inviting God's wrath and judgment through their corrupt behavior.

A WORD FROM THE JUDGE

The Lord's letter to Thyatira marks a shift in the language and tone of His correspondence. In the first group—the letters to Ephesus, Smyrna, and Pergamum—the churches had stayed true to the faith and had not yielded to the assaults of sin. Ephesus was characterized by loyalty to Christ and sound teaching, but was lacking love. Smyrna's loyalty to the Lord had been tested by fire, and they had faithfully persevered. Even to the compromising church of Pergamum, the Lord praises some of them for holding fast to His name.

Not so for the church in Thyatira, or for those to follow in Sardis and Laodicea. In these cities, the situations were far worse. It was no longer a small minority of the believers who were sinning. These churches were dominated by the satanic influences of false teaching and immorality, and the letters to them indicate the Lord's wrath over their impurity.

That's reflected right from the start in the letter to Thyatira, as the Lord identifies Himself as "the Son of God, who has eyes like a flame of fire, and His feet are like burnished bronze" (Rev. 2:18). In each letter, Christ borrows imagery from John's initial vision that ties to the nature of His message to the church. To Ephesus, He emphasized His authority and care for the church (2:1). For Smyrna, He reminded them of His eternal nature, His sacrifice on their behalf, and the glories that awaited them in heaven (v. 8). And in bringing a firm rebuke to Pergamum, He identified the power of His Word and the consequences to come if they failed to repent (v. 12).

His self-description to Thyatira similarly foreshadows His message to the church. Here He is characterized by His "eyes like a flame of fire," which signify His perfect omniscience. There was nothing going on in the church at Thyatira that He did not know about, no secret sin that had escaped His notice (see Matt. 10:26). It was a reminder that "there is no creature hidden from His sight," but that "all things are open and laid bare to the eyes of Him with whom we have to do" (Heb. 4:13). Nothing can be hidden from the eyes of the Lord.

Along with His penetrating, laser-like gaze, Christ describes His feet "like burnished bronze"—a depiction of His authority and judgment over His church. That imagery will come up again later in Revelation, when John describes the Lord's wrath poured out against the unrepentant world. He writes that Christ "treads the wine press of the fierce wrath of God, the Almighty" (Rev. 19:15). Here, the Lord's feet glow "like burnished bronze" as He tramples the impurity festering within His church.

There is one notable difference from the wording of John's original vision. John writes that he "saw one like a son of man" (1:13), emphasizing not only Christ's humanity, but also His compassion and care for His people. It reflects His intercessory work on our behalf and His understanding of our weaknesses, failures, and struggles. In Revelation 2:18, Christ instead refers to Himself as "the Son of God." This is an affirmation of His deity, and with it, His transcendence, holiness, and judgment. The Savior has become the Judge; the Intercessor becomes the executioner. Divine wrath is about to be unleashed against this idolatrous, immoral congregation. This is not comforting or sympathetic; this is threatening and fearful. This is a letter no church wants to receive.

However, like all churches, Thyatira is home to a mixture of believers and false believers. Like Pergamum, the believers were guilty of tolerating the false believers and their corrupting influence in their midst. But unlike Pergamum, false believers and idolaters *dominated* the church at Thyatira. True Christians were a scant minority.

To those faithful few, the Lord writes, "I know your deeds, and your love and faith and service and perseverance, and that your deeds of late are greater than at first" (2:19). Just as the Lord's penetrating eyes saw all the sin in the church, He assures the believers in Thyatira that He sees their faithfulness, too. Specifically, He points to their "love and faith and service and perseverance." There is no mention of the soundness of their doctrine—we don't know how wise or theologically astute these believers were. It's possible that these were still young Christians, not yet mature in their faith. But they were strong in the area that Ephesus was weak: they loved God and served each other out of that love. Christ also commends their faith and perseverance, and He notes that these godly traits were growing "greater than at first."

The church at Thyatira was an immoral cesspool, but these precious few believers were remaining faithful. In a situation like that, there is no greater comfort than knowing God sees your deeds and approves.

THE RAVAGES OF JEZEBEL

With that brief word of commendation out of the way, the Lord launches a scathing rebuke for the church at Thyatira: "But I have this against you, that you tolerate the woman Jezebel, who calls herself a prophetess, and she teaches and leads My bond-servants astray so that they commit acts of immorality and eat things sacrificed to idols" (Rev. 2:20).

Despite the undue emphasis the world has put on the word in recent years, nowhere in Scripture is the church called to be "tolerant." In fact, you could make a case that God intends for the church to be known by its *intolerance*. He demands a church that won't tolerate false teaching and immorality. He demands, as we have already seen, a church that won't tolerate sin. Thyatira was failing in those respects. The Lord says, "You tolerate the woman Jezebel, who calls herself a prophetess." The congregation at Thyatira had succumbed to some sort of first-century feminism and abdicated some level of influence in the church to a woman, contrary to the clear principle set forth by the apostle Paul in 1 Timothy 2:12: "I do not allow a woman to teach or exercise authority over a man." The Thyatiran "Jezebel" was an immoral, idolatrous woman to boot. Christ notes that she "calls herself a prophetess," which means she blasphemously claimed that her profane heresies were from God.

Scripture doesn't tell us who this woman was. Christ refers to her as "Jezebel," but that is undoubtedly not her real name. You don't find a lot of mothers choosing the name Jezebel for their baby girls. The original Jezebel was an Old Testament character—the wife of king Ahab. She was so evil and destructive that Scripture points to their marriage as the pinnacle of Ahab's wickedness: "Ahab the son of Omri did evil in the sight of the LORD more than all who were before him. It came about, as though it had been a trivial thing for him to walk in the sins of Jeroboam the son of Nebat, that he married Jezebel the daughter of Ethbaal king of the Sidonians, and went to serve Baal and worshiped him" (1 Kings 16:30–31). Baal was a Canaanite god associated with rainstorms and fertility; the rituals of his worship included self-mutilation and perverse orgies. Israel had been guilty of worshiping Baal in the past, but under Jezebel and Ahab, it became an officially sanctioned religion. As a result, Jezebel's name became synonymous with the worst evils of false religion, as well as the corruption of God's people.

We need only consider the gruesome details surrounding her death to get a sense of how God's wrath burned against this vile woman:

> When Jehu came to Jezreel, Jezebel heard of it, and she painted her eyes and adorned her head and looked out the window. As Jehu entered the gate, she said, "Is it well, Zimri, your master's murderer?" Then he lifted up his face to the window and said, "Who is on my side? Who?" And two or three officials looked down at him.
>
> He said, "Throw her down." So they threw her down, and some of her blood was sprinkled on the wall and on the horses, and he trampled her under foot. When he came in, he ate and drank; and he said, "See now to this cursed woman and bury her, for she is a king's daughter." They went to bury her, but they found nothing more of her than the skull and the feet and the palms of her hands. Therefore they returned and told him. And he said, "This is the word of the LORD, which He spoke by His servant Elijah the Tishbite, saying, 'In the property of Jezreel the dogs shall eat the flesh of Jezebel; and the corpse of Jezebel will be as dung on the face of the field in the property of Jezreel, so they cannot say, "This is Jezebel."'"
>
> (2 KINGS 9:30–37)

Like the Old Testament Jezebel, the prophetess in Thyatira was leading God's people into idolatry: "She teaches and leads My bond-servants astray so that they commit acts of immorality and eat things sacrificed to idols" (Rev. 2:20). Through her blasphemous false teaching, this woman was leading slaves of Christ back toward the bondage of paganism. Scripture tells us how seriously God takes it when a false teacher leads one of His children into immorality and heresy:

> "Whoever causes one of these little ones who believe in Me to stumble, it would be better for him to have a heavy millstone hung around his neck, and to be drowned in the depth of the sea. Woe to the world because of its stumbling blocks! For it is inevitable that stumbling blocks come; but woe to that man through whom the stumbling block comes."
> (MATT. 18:6–7)

Scripture doesn't tell us specifically what this Jezebel was teaching in the church at Thyatira—just the results of her heresy. Taking what we know about some of the false teaching that assaulted first-century believers, we can get a sense of how she lowered the spiritual defenses of the church and led the Thyatirans into such grave sin and error. The fact is those same lies still circulate to this day, with a similar corrupting effect.

It could be that the church at Thyatira succumbed to an early form of Gnostic heresy. The term *Gnosticism* comes from the Greek word for knowledge (*gnōsis*). It was a dualistic philosophy that plagued the early church. They taught that the physical universe was inherently evil while the spiritual world was good, and that salvation was simply about attaining a kind of esoteric spiritual knowledge. The result of this dualism was a total indifference to moral values and ethical behavior. Because the body and the spirit were completely distinct, sin committed in the body had no effect on the spirit. By arguing that what one did with the body didn't matter to God, adherents gave license to all sorts of fleshly iniquity.

While Gnosticism has not survived as a defined movement, gnostic ideas have resurfaced and plagued the church across the centuries. The false notion that salvation is simply a function of mental assent still plagues the church. Gnostic teaching allowed for a radical disjunction between what people say they believe and how they live their lives. That same inconsistency is pandemic in the church today. Countless people in supposedly evangelical churches believe they are saved simply because they walked an aisle and prayed a prayer to "receive Christ." They are assured of their salvation regardless of how (or whether) their supposed salvation manifests itself in their lives. Proponents of such easy-believism make the same fundamental error as the Gnostics: if you say you believe the right things, it doesn't matter how you live. The result is a false assurance of salvation that tragically leads many people to hell.

Another closely related ancient lie that might have aided the Thyatiran Jezebel's deception is known as *antinomianism*. That name comes from the Greek words for "against law" (*anti nomos*), and that's a simple way to sum up their philosophy. Antinomians believed that God's law did not apply to Christians—that His forgiveness was complete and that His grace covered any sins they had committed or would still commit in the future. They twisted the truth that "if you are led by the Spirit, you are not under the Law" (Gal. 5:18) to suggest that the law of God therefore has no relevance to Christians. With regard to the question of Romans 6:1—"What shall we say then? Are we to continue in sin so that grace may increase?"—their answer, in effect, was *Yes. Sin magnifies God's grace, so it's nothing to be concerned about.* This gross misconstrual of divine mercy gave them a callous view of righteousness and self-discipline, and led to lawless lives of open sin. Jude described and warned about those who propagated such error: "Ungodly persons who turn the grace of our God into licentiousness and deny our only Master and Lord, Jesus Christ" (Jude 4).

While the name "antinomian" remains a pejorative in Christian circles, a similarly skewed view of God's grace has been rising in popularity in recent years. Some pastors proudly flaunt their sinfulness before their congregations; others openly mock the pursuit of holiness and godliness as a legalistic denial of grace. And while the strong emphasis on God's grace may sound good initially, this theology leads to a dangerous underestimation of sin and a lack of appreciation for its true offense to God. In many cases, it is little more than a façade used to cover an immoral life.

You can see how both lies would have played into the hands of the Thyatiran Jezebel. Virtually any excuse to overlook sin would have aided her campaign of corruption. Whatever the nature of her doctrinal lies, she succeeded in convincing much of the church that the extreme immorality of paganism was acceptable behavior for believers. They believed they could claim the name of Christ while still openly indulging in the sins of the flesh. In fact, Christ's letter refers to the efforts of some in the church to "[know] the deep things of Satan, as they call them" (Rev. 2:24). Apparently this woman and her followers were not satisfied with garden-variety idolatry and paganism. They ventured deep into Satan's domain to satisfy their immoral appetites. In their twisted logic, even demonic perversions and satanically licentious behavior were permissible.

In verse 21, the Lord says, "I gave her time to repent, and she does not want to repent of her immorality." There can be no mistake— this false prophetess knew the depths of her wicked deception. She knew that her teaching was an affront to God, a blasphemy of His name, and a spiritual poison to the church. God's patience with her was now at an end, and judgment was coming.

PROCLAMATION OF DOOM

Christ promises a swift and terrible response to the corruption of His church: "Behold, I will throw her on a bed of sickness, and those who commit adultery with her into great tribulation, unless they repent of her deeds. And I will kill her children with pestilence, and all the churches will know that I am He who searches the minds and hearts; and I will give to each one of you according to your deeds" (Rev. 2:22–23).

Divine judgment was coming speedily for the Jezebel of Thyatira, and all "who commit adultery with her." Throughout Scripture, "adultery" is frequently used as a reference to spiritual infidelity. The term is fitting, and often literally applicable, because acts of fornication were deemed religious rites in many varieties of pagan religion, ranging from the ancient Canaanites to first-century Greek and Roman cults. Corinth, for example, was a city filled with temples. But brothels were even more numerous than the temples, and prostitutes served as "priestesses" of the various cults. The fact that Christ calls this Thyatiran woman "Jezebel" indicates that she and her false teaching had fostered a wicked tolerance of immoral relationships within the church. She had apparently incited physical acts of adultery within the church, mimicking the paganism of that corrupt age. The idea that this woman was guilty of actual adultery is reinforced by Christ's warning that He would "throw her on a bed." (The words "of sickness" do not appear in the original Greek text; they were added by translators.) The sense is that she and all those who partook in her iniquity would be cast into hell together.

The Lord continues, "And I will kill her children with pestilence" (v. 23). Literally translated, He says, "I will kill her children with *death*." This is most likely not a reference to any biological children she might have had. Rather, the Thyatiran Jezebel had wielded influence in the church long enough to have a second generation of followers who advocated her heresy. In order to purify His church, the Lord threatens to kill these disciples of Jezebel's debauchery.

Christ's words here ought to make a compromising, sin-tolerating pastor panic! For the sake of the purity of His church, He will kill those who bring a corrupting influence. He did it when Ananias and Sapphira lied to the Holy Spirit (Acts 5:1–11). He struck down some in the Corinthian church who abused the Lord's Supper (1 Cor. 11:28–29). First John 5:16 says there is "a sin leading to death"—a sin so serious the Lord takes the person's life. If the purity of the church is under threat, the Lord will remove that threat from the face of the earth. He may not always do it when we expect—He often extends great patience, the way He did with this Thyatiran Jezebel. But that patience isn't guaranteed. Again, we must not imagine that there is an "acceptable" amount of sin in the church. The Lord doesn't tolerate any; we shouldn't, either.

In His time, the Lord will move in decisive judgment against those corrupting His church—and not just for the sake of that individual church. Christ says He will pour out His wrath so that "all the churches will know that I am He who searches the minds and hearts; and I will give to each one of you according to your deeds" (v. 23). Put simply, the Lord was going to make an example out of Thyatira.

I don't understand how pastors and churches can be indifferent to sin when they see this unequivocal statement from the Head of the church: that He will put on a public display of His holy wrath if a church falls into corruption. He will make a spectacle of His judgment, such that other congregations see it and cringe. He will use the failure and the destruction of one church to purify others, and to display His holiness to His people. There is no excuse for tolerating sin or welcoming it as an evangelistic strategy. Doing so invites the wrath of heaven.

Christ's words in verse 23 echo Jeremiah 17:10: "I, the Lord, search the heart, I test the mind, even to give to each man according to his ways, according to the results of his deeds." This is another affirmation of His deity and authority. He reminds us that He is the omniscient Judge who sees everything with penetrating, perfect clarity.

There is, finally, a note of encouragement in His words—not for the immoral idolaters corrupting His church, but for that minority who have remained faithful against the onslaughts of Satan and his false teachers. Just as He sees the deeds of the wicked, He also sees the faithfulness of the remnant. And He doesn't close His letter without a final word of comfort to those who hold fast to the truth.

COMFORT FOR THE UNCORRUPTED

If you were a faithful believer in Thyatira, there was only one church in town. There was this church that was openly practicing idolatry, or nothing. That was your church.

Plenty of believers today feel similarly stuck in communities where there are no strong or faithful churches, where they can only search for the best of some bad options. To those faithful Christians holding on in weak and failing churches, the Lord has this to say:

> "But I say to you, the rest who are in Thyatira, who do not hold to this teaching, who have not known the deep things of Satan, as they call them—I place no other burden on you. Nevertheless what you have, hold fast until I come. He who overcomes, and he who keeps My deeds until the end, to him I will give authority over the nations; and he shall rule them with a rod of iron, as the vessels of the potter are broken to pieces, as I also have received authority from My Father; and I will give him the morning star. He who has an ear, let him hear what the Spirit says to the churches."
> (REV. 2:24–29)

The Lord always knows His own. Amidst the vile corruption in Thyatira, within a church sprinting to hell, there were still some faithful believers. The Lord saw their deeds, too. There is no other burden on them; they just need to stay faithful. They were already bearing the burden of constant false teaching; the immense weight of grief from living faithfully alongside that horrifying spectacle. That was enough. But Christ tells them they need to "hold fast" to the truth, withstanding the corrupting influences all around them. They must continue to resist the solicitations of Satan and the wicked influence of his false teachers. There is no other church to run to. They have to hold up under the pressure of this consuming corruption and wait for the Lord's purifying work to commence.

That should be a comfort to every faithful believer stuck in a sinful church. The Lord is not blind to your situation. He sees the corruption that surrounds you. He knows the burden you bear. He wants you to stay faithful, and He wants you to know He sees your faithfulness. You may be spiritually stranded, but you're never alone.

Moreover, to His faithful overcomers (see 1 John 5:4–5), Christ promises, "I will give authority over the nations; and he shall rule them with a rod of iron, as the vessels of the potter are broken to pieces, as I also have received authority from My Father" (Rev. 2:26–27). The language here comes from the words of Psalm 2:7–9: "I will surely tell of the decree of the LORD: He said to Me, 'You are My Son, today I have begotten You. Ask of Me, and I will surely give the nations as Your inheritance, and the very ends of the earth as Your possession. You shall break them with a rod of iron, You shall shatter them like earthenware.'"

This is a reference to Christ's reign in His millennial kingdom. To those who faithfully overcome, who persevere to the end, Christ promises to share His holy authority with them. The Lord will rule over the rebellious nations with a rod of iron, but He will also shepherd His people. That's the role He shares with His blessed overcomers in His kingdom.

There's more: "And I will give him the morning star" (Rev. 2:28). In Revelation 22:16, John tells us that the morning star is none other than Christ Himself: "I, Jesus, have sent My angel to testify to you these things for the churches. I am the root and the descendant of David, the bright morning star." On this side of heaven,

Christians have Christ in part. We have His Spirit indwelling us; we have His Word. This is a promise of our future relationship with Him, when we will know Christ fully, intimately, and thoroughly in the glory of His kingdom. Eagerly anticipating that blessed day, Paul wrote, "For now we see in a mirror dimly, but then face to face; now I know in part, but then I will know fully just as I also have been fully known" (1 Cor. 13:12). Overcomers will receive both the kingdom and the King.

Christ closes His letter to Thyatira with His repeated charge to the wider audience: "He who has an ear, let him hear what the Spirit says to the churches" (Rev. 2:29). The church needs to hear His words to Thyatira and tremble. We need to know that God will not be mocked, and He will not withhold His judgment indefinitely. He will fiercely punish those who tolerate and toy with sin, infecting His church with worldly corruption. But to those who withstand and remain faithful—to those who remain uncorrupted by the world—He promises the fullness of Christ as they reign with Him.

7

The Dead Church

SARDIS

The Lord has created a vast and magnificent universe, and our finite minds can comprehend only a small fraction of it. And even what we think we see in the vast recesses of space can be deceptive. For example, a light year is the distance light is able to travel—moving at more than 186,000 miles per second—in a year. The distance works out to more than six trillion miles. So as we look up into the sky at night and gaze at the stars, we're not seeing the light they're currently producing. We're seeing light from five, ten, and even twenty years ago. In fact, we could be looking at light from decades in the past, even from stars that long ago burned out. And it could be years or even decades more before we realize the light had gone out.

Today there are many churches in a similar situation. From a distance, they shine bright and brilliant, but that light is an illusion. It's merely a reflection of the past, lingering long after any light inside the church has been extinguished by sin and false teaching. The church at Sardis was like that. From the outside, you wouldn't have known anything was wrong. But in His letter to the church in Revelation 3:1–6, the Lord pronounces it dead.

FADING GLORY

About thirty miles south of Thyatira, the city of Sardis rested in the foothills of Mount Tmolus, near the Pactolus River. The river was home to large deposits of gold, which made Sardis one of the richest cities in the ancient world. It was the capital of the Lydian empire, whose king Croesus is still a benchmark for wealth ("As rich as Croesus"). In fact, Sardis is reported to be the city that first minted gold and silver into coins. Tradition tells us that Sardis also first developed the process for dying wool; textiles continued to be a major industry for the city through the first century.

A city of such vast wealth had to be able to protect itself. Sardis stood fifteen hundred feet up into the hills, surrounded by sheer cliffs and hillsides, with only a steep path that led into the city. The city was thought to be impregnable. And it might have been, if not for the carelessness of men:

> Despite an alleged warning against self-satisfaction by the Greek god whom he consulted, Croesus the king of Lydia initiated an attack against Cyrus king of Persia, but was soundly defeated. Returning to Sardis to recoup and rebuild his army for another attack, he was pursued quickly by Cyrus who laid siege against Sardis. Croesus felt utterly secure in his impregnable situation atop the acropolis and foresaw an easy victory over the Persians who were cornered among the perpendicular rocks in the lower city, an easy prey for the assembling Lydian army to crush. After retiring one evening while the drama was unfolding, he awakened to discover that the Persians had gained control of the acropolis by scaling one-by-one the

steep walls (549 B.C.). So secure did the Sardians feel that they left this means of access completely unguarded, permitting the climbers to ascend unobserved. It is said that even a child could have defended the city from this kind of attack, but not so much as one observer had been appointed to watch the side that was believed to be inaccessible.

History repeated itself more than three and a half centuries later when Antiochus the Great conquered Sardis by utilizing the services of a sure-footed mountain climber from Crete (195 B.C.). His army entered the city by another route while the defenders in careless confidence were content to guard the one known approach, the isthmus of land connected to Mount Tmolus on the south.[1]

Sardis came under Roman rule more than a hundred years before the birth of Christ. In AD 17, it was leveled by a massive earthquake that collapsed the city into rubble. The Roman Emperor Tiberius rebuilt the city, and, in return, Sardis became home to a temple in his honor. However, the city's primary deity was the goddess Cybele. The ruins of Sardis still remain today, near the village of Sart in Turkey.

While the city continued to prosper under Rome, it never returned to its former glory. In fact, it was a degenerating city, home to a degenerate church. Scripture doesn't give us any details on the founding of the church at Sardis. It likely got its start during Paul's ministry in Ephesus (Acts 19:10).

Christ's letter to the church at Sardis stands out in some ways for what it *doesn't say*. There is no mention of persecution. There's no mention of bad theology or false teachers. There's no discussion of compromise with the world or any specific sin corrupting the church. But we can reasonably assume that all those were issues for the congregation at Sardis; that they were further down the spiritual slide the Lord has been describing. In fact, He says the worst thing that could be said about a church: it's dead. In less than forty years, they had left their first love like Ephesus, were seduced by compromise like Pergamum, and had succumbed to corruption like Thyatira. How else could they have so rapidly descended into the kind of spiritual decay the Lord describes in Revelation?

THE DIVINE SOLUTION TO DESPERATE NEEDS

In His letter to Sardis, Christ identifies Himself in a compelling way, as "He who has the seven Spirits of God and the seven stars" (Rev. 3:1). As we've seen, Christ borrows imagery from John's initial vision to illustrate specific aspects of His character that reinforce His words to each particular church. But the reference to the "seven Spirits of God" points back further, to John's own greeting to the seven churches in Revelation 1:4: "John to the seven churches that are in Asia: Grace to you and peace, from Him who is and who was and who is to come, and from the seven Spirits who are before His throne." It's a phrase he uses repeatedly throughout the book (see also 4:5; 5:6). But what does it mean, since there is only one Holy Spirit (Eph. 4:4)?

There are two ways to understand the imagery here. First, we can look back at Isaiah 11:2, where Isaiah describes the Holy Spirit's relationship to the Messiah. He writes, "The Spirit of the LORD will rest on Him, the spirit of wisdom and understanding, the spirit of counsel and strength, the spirit of knowledge and the fear of the LORD." Isaiah identifies seven key features of the Spirit's empowering work: He is the Spirit of the Lord as well as the spirit of wisdom, understanding, counsel, strength, knowledge, and the fear of the Lord. This is what is commonly referred to as the sevenfold Spirit of the Lord; it's a way to understand the Spirit in the fullness of His power and work.

The other way to understand what Christ means when He says

He "has the seven Spirits of God" is to see a reference to Zechariah's prophetic vision of the Holy Spirit as a golden lampstand made up of seven lamps in Zechariah 4:1–10. In either case, this is a certain reference to the Holy Spirit, who was given to the church by Christ.

So, to the church at Sardis, the Lord describes Himself as the one who possesses the Holy Spirit in His fullness, and the "seven stars"—a reference to John's initial vision (Rev. 1:16) that depicts the Lord's sovereign care for the messengers to the seven churches. In short, the Author of the letter is the one who gives the Holy Spirit to the church, and who sovereignly leads the church through His shepherds.

How does that relate to the congregation at Sardis? Why isn't He coming in omniscient judgment, with eyes of fire and feet of bronze? As we'll see, there's not much judgment in this letter, because the church is already dead from the start.

Christ describes Himself as the One who possesses what this church needs most: the Holy Spirit and faithful shepherds. The church at Sardis had neither. They were devoid of the Holy Spirit and without spiritually qualified pastors. There was no godly leadership; the church was being led astray by men who did not know and love the truth. The life and power of the Holy Spirit was not there. The illuminating, enabling work of the Spirit had all but ceased. Without the Holy Spirit and without faithful leaders, the church was dead. It was a church dominated by the flesh, sin, and unbelief—and mostly populated by the unregenerate. The church at Sardis had desperate spiritual needs that only Christ could meet.

THE DEEDS OF THE DEAD

The Lord's pattern in these letters has been to include some words of commendation or praise up front for those in the churches who have remained faithful to Him and His Word. His letter to Sardis breaks that pattern. He writes, "I know your deeds, that you have a name that you are alive, but you are dead" (Rev. 3:1).

Our God is omniscient; He sees everything and He sees *through* everything. The church at Sardis looked fine to the naked eye. Christ says they "have a name that you are alive, but you are dead." He could see through the façade of their deeds to the true nature of their hearts. This isn't merely physical death He's talking about— they're spiritually dead. It's what Paul describes in Ephesians 2:1 as "dead in your trespasses and sins." In Colossians 2:13, he writes, "You were dead in your transgressions and the uncircumcision of your flesh." That's the kind of death the Lord is describing in Sardis. He can see that this church is unsaved, that it might as well be the world.

Sadly, we see a lot of churches like that today. The world is full of liberal churches that don't believe the Bible is the Word of God. They deny the deity and atoning work of Christ; they deny His gospel. They still go through the motions of piety and the forms of worship, but there is no spiritual life inside. Pretended devotion to Christ is a sham; there's no drive to see the unregenerate saved because they themselves are unregenerate, too.

In a sense, it is easy to spot a dead church. It's a church that's wrapped up in religious tradition practiced by rote but devoid of real faith. It's concerned with liturgy and form, but not true worship. It's a church consumed with healing social ills and promoting public welfare, but not preaching the power of the gospel to transform lives. It's a church that tolerates sin rather than confronting it. It's a church that is more interested in the fashions and opinions of men than the Word of God. It's a church devoted to material things, even vaguely spiritual things, but not the Scripture in its fullness. It's a church that has no desire for holiness.

And only thirty or forty years after it was founded—from the time the gospel exploded throughout Asia Minor (see Acts 19:10) to John's exile on Patmos—the church at Sardis had died. Such rapid decay is a warning in itself.

What could kill a church so quickly? Error kills the church. False teaching and false doctrine confuse and corrupt the church, draining the life out of it. Sin kills the church. Little by little, sin tears away at the life of the church. It twists your character and warps your mind. Sins of omission and commission slowly suffocate the will of the church to maintain holiness and purity. Sinful leadership can quickly deal death blows to a church. Compromise with the world kills the church, too. Contrary to the current trend, there's no better way to introduce the killing power of sin into a church than with an influx of unbelievers. Accepting and putting those unbelievers into positions of leadership grips the church by the neck and strangles it. Ultimately, churches die for one reason: they tolerate sin, which includes the seminal sin of not taking Scripture seriously.

Evidently, the church at Sardis was still going through religious motions. Maybe they helped with some of the city's social ills; maybe they did some philanthropic work or provided services to the community. But the Lord says, "I know your deeds." At the end of Revelation 3:2, He adds, "I have not found your deeds completed in the sight of My God." That's another way to say their deeds are unsatisfactory. Their pious pantomime wasn't fooling the Lord; their good works were unacceptable. The church might have been socially distinguished, but they were living a lie. Inside it was a spiritual graveyard, and their good works were a poor disguise for an ecclesiastical corpse.

In that sense, they were a lot like Samson. In the dark days of Israel's history, in the time of the Judges, the Lord gave Samson as a champion to the Israelites to fight the Philistines. He was a lovable hero for God's people, performing miraculous feats of strength and heroic exploits that every Sunday school child knows by heart.

But Samson fell into sin. He succumbed to lust and pride, and foolishly divulged the secret of his strength: his hair. Ultimately, it was not the haircut that cost him his strength, but the fact that he broke a vow to God. When the Philistines attacked him again,

Scripture tells us he was easily captured because "he did not know that the LORD had departed from him. Then the Philistines seized him and gouged out his eyes; and they brought him down to Gaza and bound him with bronze chains, and he was a grinder in the prison" (Judg. 16:20–21).

What a tragic statement: "he did not know that the LORD had departed from him." His sin turned him into a miserable wreck— blind, pitiful, and imprisoned, slaving over the grinding mill in chains for the remainder of his life. That was the church at Sardis. At one point they had been alive and powerful, but they began to court the world and tolerate sin. Over time, they became weak and blind, unaware that God had departed from their midst.

So many churches today are the same. They're dressed up and organized. They give every outward appearance of life. But inside the whole congregation is blind and bound in the chains of their sin. To churches like that, the Lord says, "You have a name that you are alive, but you are dead."

MOSTLY DEAD

Christ's commands to the church reveal that there was still some vague spiritual life in Sardis. He says, "Wake up, and strengthen the things that remain, which were about to die; for I have not found your deeds completed in the sight of My God. So remember what you have received and heard; and keep it, and repent. Therefore if you do not wake up, I will come like a thief, and you will not know at what hour I will come to you" (Rev. 3:2–3). There's no use telling a dead man to wake up.

So the Lord speaks to those few remaining believers in Sardis. He gives them five commands to rescue the church from its death spiral and prompt the necessary reformation and restoration in Sardis.

The first is simply to "wake up" (v. 2). This was no time for spiritual lethargy. They needed to shrug off their spiritual indifference and leap to action. It's a call to look around and accurately assess the situation. There could be no more passive acceptance of the status quo. The church was dying; much of it was already dead. Wake up and be alert. It's time to work.

His second command is to "strengthen the things that remain, which were about to die" (v. 2). This is a call to rescue what they can from the dying church. To peel back the years of dry rot and decay and salvage whatever they could of its former spiritual value. Any virtue and godliness that still remained, any embers of their love for Christ that could still be fanned—strengthen those things.

In verse 3, Christ commanded them to "remember what you have received and heard." By this point, the New Testament canon was closing. All the Gospels and epistles had been written. We know Paul's letters were circulating through the church (see 2 Peter 3:15–16); certainly others were as well. The Lord is telling any remaining believers in Sardis to think back on the spiritual truth they had received and not let their hearts grow cold to His Word. In effect, "Remember the truth of Christ's glorious gospel; remember the teaching that the apostles suffered and died to deliver to you." This is similar to Paul's charge to Timothy: "Guard what has been entrusted to you" (1 Tim. 6:20). The believers in Sardis had to recover the preciousness of God's Word if they hoped to revive and rescue their dying church.

But it's not enough to merely remember the truth. Christ also commanded that they "keep it" (Rev. 3:3). Like we saw in the church at Pergamum, it's not enough to know the truth. The Lord commands us to obey it as well. Remembering the truth would not help the church if they were not living it out.

Finally, the Lord ordered them to "repent" (v. 3). On top of everything else, those in the Sardis church needed to confess their sins and turn from them. Without repentance, none of the other changes would have lasted or made a lasting difference in the life of the church. They had to break with any patterns of sinfulness and come to a right relationship with God if there was going to be true revival in the church.

And the Lord warned them what would happen if they failed to fulfill His commands: "Therefore if you do not wake up, I will come like a thief, and you will not know at what hour I will come to you" (v. 3). When the Lord talks about coming like a thief, it's a picture of His imminent judgment. It means He is coming without warning, when they least expect it. Later in Revelation 16:15, we read, "Behold, I am coming like a thief. Blessed is the one who stays awake and keeps his clothes, so that he will not walk about naked and men will not see his shame." In his second epistle, Peter warns, "The day of the Lord will come like a thief, in which the heavens will pass away with a roar and the elements will be destroyed with intense heat, and the earth and its works will be burned up" (2 Peter 3:10). That's a warning of God's final judgment on the world. Christ's words to Sardis are a much more localized promise of doom. If the church does not repent and reform, He will come at an unknown moment to bring mayhem and destruction upon them.

This same threat applies to all dead churches. If they fail to wake up from their spiritual slumber, strengthen their love for God, remember the truth of His Word, live lives of obedience, and repent of their sins, they face the horror and terror Paul described in 1 Thessalonians 5:2–3: "For you yourselves know full well that the day of the Lord will come just like a thief in the night. While they are saying, 'Peace and safety!' then destruction will come upon them suddenly like labor pains upon a woman with child, and they will not escape."

TO THOSE WITH UNSOILED GARMENTS

The Lord closes His letter to Sardis with an encouragement to the small group of faithful believers who remained: "But you have a few people in Sardis who have not soiled their garments; and they will walk with Me in white, for they are worthy" (Rev. 3:4). In the midst of this dead church were a precious few who had not followed the church into sin and spiritual decay. There were a few genuine believers among the hypocrites, a few separated and spiritual among the carnal and the worldly. The Lord had a small remnant of true Christians, leading pure, wholesome, Christlike lives in the midst of this dead, corrupt church.

In Romans 11:1–5, Paul reminds his readers that God will always have a remnant of His people Israel, no matter how dire and spiritually dead the nation appears:

> I say then, God has not rejected His people, has He? May it never be! For I too am an Israelite, a descendant of Abraham, of the tribe of Benjamin. God has not rejected His people whom He foreknew. Or do you not know what the Scripture says in the passage about Elijah, how he pleads with God against Israel? "Lord, they have killed Your prophets, they have torn down Your altars, and I alone am left, and they are seeking my life." But what is the divine response to him? "I have kept for Myself seven thousand men who have not bowed the knee to Baal." In the same way then, there has also come to be at the present time a remnant according to God's gracious choice.

Evidently, the number of faithful believers in Sardis was miniscule; it was small enough not to impact the Lord's evaluation that the church as a whole was dead. But that did not mean that the Lord would forget or ignore those faithful few that had carried on in love for the truth and perseverance. As the author of Hebrews reminds us, "For God is not unjust so as to forget your work and the love which you have shown toward His name, in having ministered and in still ministering to the saints" (Heb. 6:10).

The Lord did not forget His people in Sardis; in fact, He memorialized their faithfulness to every generation of the church in His letter. He says they "have not soiled their garments" (Rev. 3:4). Translated literally, the word (*moluno*) means stained or dyed. In Scripture, garments are often used to refer to the spiritual character of a person. Jude 23, for instance, describes the spiritual contamination of people corrupted by false teachers as "the garment polluted by the flesh." These unsoiled garments represent the godly character and purity of these few believers—all the more remarkable when you consider the corruption of their church.

Christ says this faithful remnant "will walk with Me in white, for they are worthy" (Rev. 3:4). White robes, like the ones Christ describes here, were commonly worn at celebrations and festivals, or after military victories. Even pagans would come to worship their false gods in clean, white clothes as a symbol of their goodness and virtue. They wanted to present themselves as worthy of the idol's affection and good will. But these aren't merely clean robes in this temporal world. Christ is referring to the bright, gleaming spiritual robes of imputed righteousness, covering believers who have been purified by His sacrifice on their behalf. In Revelation 7:14, we read of those who "have washed their robes and made them white in the blood of the Lamb."

This is the glorious truth of the gospel. In Romans 5:19, Paul says, "For as through one man's disobedience the many were made sinners, even so through the obedience of the One the many will be made righteous." Just as we were made sinners through Adam's sin, we have been made righteous through Christ's death. How? Paul proclaims the reality in 2 Corinthians: "He made Him who knew no sin to be sin on our behalf, so that we might become the righteousness of God in Him" (5:21). On the cross, God treated Christ as if He had lived my life of sin, so that He could treat me as if I had lived Christ's life of righteousness. As new creations in Christ, we are cloaked in His righteousness. When God looks at us now, He sees only the holy perfection of His Son.

The imagery of soiled garments is a thread that runs through Scripture. Because we are fallen creatures, hopelessly defiled by our own sin, even the righteous deeds we do cannot cover our sins. Indeed, "All of us have become like one who is unclean, and all our righteous deeds are like a filthy garment" (Isa. 64:6). The very best things we do are still tainted by sin. Thus, anyone who expects to stand before God clothed in the "righteousness" of his or her own good works is trusting a garment that is polluted by the flesh.

God demands *perfect* righteousness. Jesus said, "Unless your righteousness surpasses that of the scribes and Pharisees, you will not enter the kingdom of heaven" (Matt. 5:20). How high is the standard? "You are to be perfect, as your heavenly Father is perfect" (v. 48).

That sets an unattainable standard. But Christ provides a perfect righteousness by imputation for all who truly trust Him as Lord and Savior. God imputes righteousness to believers apart from any good works that they do (Rom. 4:6). The righteousness of Christ covers them like a gleaming-white, spotless garment of absolute perfection. In the words of Isaiah 61:10, "I will rejoice greatly in the LORD, My soul will exult in my God; for He has clothed me with garments of salvation, He has wrapped me with a robe of righteousness." That's what the apostle Paul meant when he testified that he had come to be, by faith, "Found in [Christ], not having a righteousness of my own derived from the Law, but that which is through faith in Christ, the righteousness which comes from God on the basis of faith" (Phil. 3:9).

Subsequently, the process of sanctification is progressively purifying believers to make them more and more Christlike. We "are being transformed into the same image from glory to glory, just as from the Lord, the Spirit" (2 Cor. 3:18). One day, when we go to be with Christ, or when He returns to take us from this world, our glorification will be instantly complete: "Beloved, now we are children of God, and it has not appeared as yet what we will be.

We know that when He appears, we will be like Him, because we will see Him just as He is" (1 John 3:2).

These are the robes John describes the church wearing at the marriage supper of the Lamb: "'Let us rejoice and be glad and give glory to Him, for the marriage of the Lamb has come and His bride has made herself ready.' It was given to her to clothe herself in fine linen, bright and clean; for the fine linen is the righteous acts of the saints" (Rev. 19:7–8).

The small remnant in Sardis had not fallen into pagan impurities. They had not succumbed to sinful practices. They were in a dead church but were alive spiritually. And for their faithfulness, they would walk with their Savior in eternal holiness.

DIVINE BOOKKEEPING AND ETERNAL SECURITY

Christ continues this theme in His words to the wider audience of His letter: "He who overcomes will thus be clothed in white garments" (Rev. 3:5). He promises that faithful believers who persevere to the end will be cloaked in His righteousness, and will one day be made righteous. There are no caveats or conditions here; this is Christ's faithful promise to all who overcome (see 1 John 5:4–5) and remain faithful to Him.

That's important to remember, as some have misconstrued the rest of Christ's statement. The Lord says, "And I will not erase his name from the book of life, and I will confess his name before My Father and before His angels" (Rev. 3:5). Although Christ promises *not* to erase the names of His people, some take it to mean that it *could* happen, turning God's promise into a veiled threat. That erroneous view appeals to Exodus 32:33, where "The LORD said to Moses, 'Whoever has sinned against Me, I will blot him out of My book.'"

In the ancient world, rulers of cities had a census, a record of all the names of their citizens. As a citizen, there were effectively two ways your name could be blotted out of the ledger. You could die or you could commit a crime against the state and lose your citizenship. The book the Lord referred to in Exodus was like that—it's a reference to physical death, not eternal damnation.

On the other hand, the book of life mentioned in Revelation is God's book in which He keeps record of those who have eternal life. The apostle John refers to it as the list of names "written from the foundation of the world in the book of life of the Lamb who has been slain" (Rev. 13:8; see also 17:8). God does not add and subtract names from the book of life; the names of His faithful believers are written there for eternity.

In John's vision of the future great white throne judgment, we see the end result of Christ's promise to keep our names secure:

> Then I saw a great white throne and Him who sat upon it, from whose presence earth and heaven fled away, and no place was found for them. And I saw the dead, the great and the small, standing before the throne, and books were opened; and another book was opened, which is the book of life; and the dead were judged from the things which were written in the books, according to their deeds. And the sea gave up the dead which were in it, and death and Hades gave up the dead which were in them; and they were judged, every one of them according to their deeds. Then death and Hades were thrown into the lake of fire. This is the second death, the lake of fire. And if anyone's name was not found written in the book of life, he was thrown into the lake of fire.
> (REV. 20:11–15)

Christ promises each of His faithful overcomers, "I will confess his name before My Father and before His angels" (3:5). This is an echo of a promise Christ made to His disciples in Matthew 10:32: "Everyone who confesses Me before men, I will also confess him before My Father who is in heaven." There is no greater blessing than the assurance of our salvation and an eternity with our Savior.

In Romans 8, Paul recounts the unbreakable chain of God's work in salvation, and the tremendous security we enjoy in Him:

> And we know that God causes all things to work together for good to those who love God, to those who are called according to His purpose. For those whom He foreknew, He also predestined to become conformed to the image of His Son, so that He would be the firstborn among many brethren; and these whom He predestined, He also called; and these whom He called, He also justified; and these whom He justified, He also glorified.
>
> What then shall we say to these things? If God is for us, who is against us? He who did not spare His own Son, but delivered Him over for us all, how will He not also with Him freely give us all things? Who will bring a charge against God's elect? God is the one who justifies; who is the one who condemns? Christ Jesus is He who died, yes, rather who was raised, who is at the right hand of God, who also intercedes for us. Who will separate us from the love of Christ? Will tribulation, or distress, or persecution, or famine, or nakedness, or peril, or sword? Just as it is written, "For Your sake we are being put to death all day long; we were considered as sheep to be slaughtered." But in all these things we overwhelmingly conquer through Him who loved us. For I am convinced that neither death, nor life, nor angels, nor principalities, nor things present, nor things to come, nor powers, nor height, nor depth, nor any other created thing, will be able to separate us from the love of God, which is in Christ Jesus our Lord. (vv. 28–39)

Christ's letter to the dead church at Sardis is full of rich hope for His saints. He promises to clothe them in the white linens of eternal life, never erase their names out of the book of life, and personally confess them before His Father and the entire heavenly host. Those promises extend to all His beloved ones.

The Lord's letter to Sardis ends with His familiar charge to the rest of His church: "He who has an ear, let him hear what the Spirit says to the churches" (Rev. 3:6). For the believers listening, there is wonderful news to behold.

And history tells us that the church at Sardis was listening. We know of a faithful pastor and apologist from the second century named Melito. Some say he wrote the first commentary on Revelation. He served as the bishop of Sardis, which gives us reason to hope that revival came to the dead church. It seems the believers did wake up and remember the truth they had received, and perhaps some of the dead were brought to spiritual life through repentance and faith.

And we can pray that the Lord will do a similar work to revive, reform, and restore many more dead churches today.

8

The Faithful Church
PHILADELPHIA

There are no perfect churches.

That should not come as a shock to Christians, but it often does. If we're honest about our own faults and shortcomings, we know we're not perfect; no believer is. We all fall short of God's standard of absolute and complete holiness. And as a collection of imperfect Christians, the church itself cannot help but be imperfect, too.

At the same time, believers need to realize there isn't always a *better* church, either. Too many Christians have developed nomadic tendencies when it comes to a church. They're restlessly looking over the fence to see where the grass might be greener. Some constantly shift between congregations, looking for something they can't find. Maybe it's a different style of service, better music, a more convenient location, or a more affluent and energetic congregation. Not all the reasons are selfish or unbiblical; some people simply want to find a stronger, more biblical preacher or a better Sunday school program for their children.

But the inability (or unwillingness) of so many Christians to commit to a local church and stay faithful comes at a high cost. How can a pastor grow in his shepherding abilities if his sheep won't stay put? How does a church improve its worship, programs, or administration if people with any aptitude in those areas of ministry keep leaving for churches that already have them figured out? More Christians need to be willing to invest in their local churches, to look for ways to serve, sacrifice, and be part of the solution rather than bolt at the first sign of a problem.

We ought to be thankful that the Lord isn't so fickle when it comes to the church, that He doesn't withhold His blessing from struggling and imperfect congregations. He's not interested in only the most popular and polished. As we see in the letter to the church at Philadelphia, what matters to God is *faithfulness*.

THE CITY AND THE CHURCH

The ancient city of Philadelphia was located roughly thirty miles southeast of Sardis, in the Cogamis River valley. Founded less than two hundred years before the birth of Christ, it was named for Attalus II, the king of Pergamum, whose loyalty to his older brother and predecessor, King Eumenes, earned him the nickname *Philadelphus* ("brother lover").

The city was rich in agriculture—particularly its vineyards—thanks to the deposits of volcanic ash in the area. It sat on the edge of a region known as the *Katakekaumene* (the "burned land"). The soil was fertile but it came at a cost—the area was prone to volatile seismic activity. The same earthquake that leveled Sardis in AD 17 also did significant damage in Philadelphia, which was closer to the epicenter and suffered through years of aftershocks. Sir William Ramsey explains that the experience left the town skittish and scarred:

Many of the inhabitants remained outside the city living in huts and booths over the vale, and those who were foolhardy enough (as the sober-minded thought) to remain in the city, practised various devices to support and strengthen the walls and houses against the recurring shocks. The memory of this disaster lived long; the very name Katakekaumene was a perpetual warning; people lived amid ever threatening danger, in dread always of a new disaster; and the habit of going out to the open country had probably not disappeared when the Seven Letters were written.[1]

Situated along an important trade route, Philadelphia was founded as a beacon of Greek culture and Hellenism in Asia Minor. It proved so influential that Greek replaced the Lydian language by AD 19. The city also showed a strong allegiance to Rome. Just as in Sardis, Philadelphia was home to a temple built in honor of the Emperor Tiberius—a show of thanks for Rome's rebuilding help after the earthquake. But Philadelphia went above and beyond in its devotion, changing its name to Neocaesarea ("New City of the Caesar") for a few years to profess its civic gratitude. Today, it is the Turkish town of Alaşehir.

Scripture doesn't tell us much about the church in Philadelphia. Like the other churches in Asia Minor, it was most likely founded during Paul's ministry in Ephesus (see Acts 19:10). We know that the early church father Ignatius visited the believers in Philadelphia on the way to his execution in Rome. He later wrote his Letter to the Philadelphians to encourage and strengthen the church. Tradition tells us that some from Philadelphia were martyred in Smyrna alongside Polycarp. And we know the church maintained a presence in Philadelphia for many centuries. It is believed to have disappeared by the fourteenth century, long after Islam's influence dominated the region.

CHRIST IN ALL HIS MAJESTY

Like His letter to the church at Smyrna, the Lord's words to the believers in Philadelphia contain no rebuke or condemnation. There are no threats here, no warnings of judgment. The letter is free from criticism of any kind. Instead, it's a note of commendation and praise for this faithful little church, and some promises of divine blessing to come.

In his exile on Patmos, the apostle John wrote under the Lord's divine inspiration. To identify His authorship of the letter, Christ describes Himself as "He who is holy, who is true, who has the key of David, who opens and no one will shut, and who shuts and no one opens" (Rev. 3:7). This is the first time in the opening of a letter that Christ has not harkened back to John's initial vision of Him in Revelation 1:12–17. Instead, He draws on some Old Testament phrases and images to assert His deity and depict His relationship to the Philadelphian church.

The phrase "He who is holy" can refer only to God. Holiness describes God's utter separation from sin; it signifies His unblemished perfection. Throughout Scripture, the holiness of God is consistently affirmed and praised. The psalmist writes, "I will praise You with a harp, even Your truth, O my God; to You I will sing praises with the lyre, O Holy One of Israel" (Ps. 71:22). In the prophet Isaiah's vision, the angels call out, "Holy, Holy, Holy is the LORD of hosts, the whole earth is full of His glory" (Isa. 6:3). The four living creatures in the throne room of heaven perpetually proclaim, "Holy, holy, holy is the Lord God, the Almighty, who was and who is and who is to come" (Rev. 4:8).

In the New Testament, references to Christ's holiness are frequently tied to His role as Messiah. The angel who announced His birth to Mary identified Him as "the holy Child" (Luke 1:35). Early in Christ's ministry, a frightened demon cried out in His presence, "What business do we have with each other, Jesus of Nazareth?

Have You come to destroy us? I know who You are—the Holy One of God!" The disciples also affirmed Christ's holiness. Peter said, "We have believed and have come to know that You are the Holy One of God" (John 6:69). In his sermon in Acts 3, Peter rebuked those who cried out for Christ's crucifixion, saying, "But you disowned the Holy and Righteous One and asked for a murderer to be granted to you" (v. 14).

Christ's assertion of His holiness in Revelation 3 affirms both His deity as the Son of God and His humanity as the Messiah. It unites Him in character and nature with the Father, and it signifies His role as incarnate Savior to the believers in Philadelphia.

That could have been a frightening introduction, because holiness cannot tolerate sin. Holiness cannot look upon iniquity or evil. In 1 Peter 1:15, the church is commanded, "Like the Holy One who called you, be holy yourselves also in all your behavior." But this was no prelude to judgment. Instead, it is the Holy One Himself who speaks well of the church in Philadelphia.

In addition to His holiness, Christ writes that He is the One "who is true" (Rev. 3:7). The Greek word here (*alēthinos*) does not refer to a true statement, but rather to One who is authentic, as opposed to someone who is a fraud. It speaks to His purity, fidelity, credibility, dependability, and genuineness. He is the true God, not a false one. He is the holy and genuine Lord, perfect in righteousness and true in His character and all that He says. Again, it's remarkable that He introduces Himself this way and that there is no condemnation to follow. He is the true God who has no place for error or falsehood, and He does not rebuke this church.

Christ further identifies Himself in verse 7 as the One "who has the key of David, who opens and no one will shut, and who shuts and no one opens." In God's Word, keys are emblematic of authority, control, and sovereignty. The language here is a direct reference to Isaiah 22:22 and the authority entrusted to the king's steward, Eliakim: "Then I will set the key of the house of David on his shoulder, when he opens no one will shut, when he shuts no one will open." As the steward, Eliakim determined who would be admitted into the king's presence and who would be denied. He also controlled access to the royal treasury and had authority to dispense its riches.

Applied to Christ, this is a reference to His absolute authority, especially over His messianic kingdom. As Peter declared in Acts 4:12, "There is salvation in no one else; for there is no other name under heaven that has been given among men by which we must be saved." Christ alone determines who gains access into His eternal kingdom. He is the ultimate authority over the riches of heaven and He pours them out according to His sovereign will.

Earlier, in Revelation 1:18, the Lord reminded the apostle John, "I have the keys of death and of Hades." Both images illustrate Christ's sovereign authority over both eternal blessing and eternal judgment. As Christ said to His disciples, "I am the way, and the truth, and the life; no one comes to the Father but through Me" (John 14:6).

This is the Lord Jesus Christ in all His majesty. He is holy and one with the Father. He is true, and there is none other like Him. He is omniscient, sovereign, and omnipotent, and the keys to eternal blessing are His alone. This is the Lord who looks at the church in Philadelphia and finds nothing to rebuke them for, nothing to condemn. This is wondrously, graciously encouraging, not because they were a perfect church—they weren't—but because they were faithful. And the Lord and Head of the church blesses faithfulness.

FOUR QUALITIES OF A FAITHFUL CHURCH

Christ made some magnificent promises to the believers in Philadelphia. But before we consider the fruits of their faithfulness, we need to see what marked them as faithful in the first place.

In Revelation 3:8, the Lord writes, "I know your deeds. . . .

[Y]ou have a little power, and have kept My word, and have not denied My name." The holy, sovereign, powerful Lord knows everything there is to know about this church. He never spells out the specifics of their deeds. All we know is that they were acceptable to the Lord, as He affirms them as a church He will bless. But He does give us some indication of what characterized this faithful congregation.

First, He says, "You have a little power." This doesn't mean it was a weak church, but that it was few in number. Their power was not limited by sin or a lack of spiritual maturity; they had "a little power" because they were a little church. It's also possible—even likely—that the church was made up of slaves and poor believers. That would fit with what Paul tells us about God's design for the church in general:

> For consider your calling, brethren, that there were not
> many wise according to the flesh, not many mighty, not
> many noble; but God has chosen the foolish things of
> the world to shame the wise, and God has chosen the
> weak things of the world to shame the things which are
> strong, and the base things of the world and the despised
> God has chosen, the things that are not, so that He may
> nullify the things that are, so that no man may boast
> before God.
> (1 COR. 1:26–29)

In fact, the Philadelphian church could say confidently with Paul, "I am well content with weaknesses, with insults, with distresses, with persecutions, with difficulties, for Christ's sake; for when I am weak, then I am strong" (2 Cor. 12:10).

The church was small, limited in number, but not in spiritual power. The implication is that they were true worshipers, true lovers of Christ, and true to the Word of God. That's further reinforced by the next characteristic of their faithfulness.

The Lord writes, "And [you] have kept My word" (Rev. 3:8).

They were bound to divine revelation. They didn't deviate from the path of obedience to the Lord. They followed the example of Job, who said, "I have not departed from the command of His lips; I have treasured the words of His mouth more than my necessary food" (Job 23:12).

Before He was arrested, Christ repeatedly stressed the importance of faithful obedience to His disciples: "He who has My commandments and keeps them is the one who loves Me. . . . If anyone loves Me, he will keep My word. . . . He who does not love Me does not keep My words" (John 14:21, 23–24). Later that evening, He promised, "If you keep My commandments, you will abide in My love" (John 15:10). In his first epistle, John presents the acid test of saving faith: "By this we know that we have come to know Him, if we keep His commandments. The one who says, 'I have come to know Him,' and does not keep His commandments, is a liar, and the truth is not in him; but whoever keeps His word, in him the love of God has truly been perfected" (1 John 2:3–5). Their love for the Lord was proven by their obedience to His Word.

They were also marked by loyalty. Christ notes that the Philadelphian believers "have not denied My name" (Rev. 3:8), implying they were under pressure to do so. The church at Pergamum was similarly commended for their loyalty to Christ: "I know where you dwell, where Satan's throne is; and you hold fast My name, and did not deny My faith even in the days of Antipas, My witness, My faithful one, who was killed among you, where Satan dwells" (2:13). Both churches faced the threat of persecution and refused to deny the Lord's name. They were loyal, regardless of what their loyalty cost them. Describing the believers during the tribulation who refuse the mark of the beast, John writes, "Here is the perseverance of the saints who keep the commandments of God and their faith in Jesus" (14:12). The Philadelphian believers were not intimidated by persecution. They stayed loyal to Christ, no matter the cost.

Finally, the Lord says the church at Philadelphia was characterized by endurance. In Revelation 3:10, He commends them, "Because you have kept the word of My perseverance." This also indicates that the church was facing persecution. But that was not unique to this particular church; it's the life of every Christian. In Matthew 10:22, Jesus warned His disciples, "You will be hated by all because of My name, but it is the one who has endured to the end who will be saved" (see also Matt. 24:13). Christ commands His people to endure faithfully against the intense hostility of the world. As an encouragement in that constant struggle, Paul wrote to another church, "May the Lord direct your hearts into the love of God and into the steadfastness of Christ" (2 Thess. 3:5). Through trials and persecution, these faithful Christians patiently endured and never wavered in their commitment to Christ.

So did the faithful in the church at Philadelphia. The power of the Holy Spirit was at work in and through them. They obeyed God's Word. They were loyal to Christ in the face of persecution. And they endured trials and hostility, proving their love for Christ. Those were the qualities that united to create their faithfulness. And those remain the qualities every church must cultivate to be known by the Lord as faithful.

DIVINE COMMITMENTS

Because of its power, obedience, loyalty, and endurance, the church at Philadelphia was given some incomparable privileges. We see the first of these divine commitments in Revelation 3:8: "I know your deeds. Behold, I have put before you an open door which no one can shut, because you have a little power, and have kept My word, and have not denied My name." This ties back to what the Lord has just said about Himself in verse 7—that He is the one "who has the key of David, who opens and no one will shut, and who shuts and no one opens." That was a reference to His sovereign control over access to His heavenly kingdom. As an extension of that idea, this is a promise that no one can shut them out of heaven, that their salvation is secure in Christ. Under the crushing weight of persecution, there is no greater comfort than to know your faith, and thus your eternity, is held fast in the omnipotent hands of the Lord. Christ Himself opens the door for His people to enter into the blessings of His heaven, and there is no force in existence that can close it.

There is likely another layer to this promise. Not only has Christ opened the door to heaven for the faithful Philadelphians; He has opened the door for them to usher others into the kingdom as well. Christ is speaking of the gospel opportunity He has blessed them with. In the Pauline epistles, an open door is often a reference to an evangelistic opportunity. Paul used the expression in both of his letters to the Corinthians. "I will remain in Ephesus until Pentecost; for a wide door for effective service has opened to me, and there are many adversaries" (1 Cor. 16:8–9). "Now when I came to Troas for the gospel of Christ and when a door was opened for me in the Lord" (2 Cor. 2:12). He used it again in Colossians 4:2–3: "Devote yourselves to prayer, keeping alert in it with an attitude of thanksgiving; praying at the same time for us as well, that God will open up to us a door for the word."

No doubt, the little church in Philadelphia had an open door, with people constantly passing through town as they traveled the ancient trade routes. The city had already heavily influenced the region with the Greek language and culture. In the same way, this church had a strategic opportunity to reach out into Asia Minor with the gospel. Their faithfulness would be rewarded with opportunities for the gospel to be given to unbelievers. They would enjoy the privilege of being used by God to lead others into the kingdom of His beloved Son.

The Lord gives them a second pledge in Revelation 3:9: "Behold, I will cause those of the synagogue of Satan, who say they are Jews and are not, but lie—I will make them come and bow down at your feet, and make them know that I have loved you." Christ previously referenced the synagogue of Satan in His letter to Smyrna (Rev. 2:9). Just like the believers there, the Philadelphian church faced strong opposition from the local Jews. Throughout the New Testament, Israel's religious leaders tried to halt the spread of the gospel. They hated Christ and anyone who held Him up as the Messiah. In their opposition to the gospel, they were doing the devil's work. Christ confronted them on that very point in John's gospel: "You are doing the deeds of your father. . . . You are of your father the devil" (John 8:41, 44). We've already seen how they hounded the apostles in the earliest days of the church. Here, at the end of the first century, the relationship had not improved.

Christ says these persecutors "say they are Jews and are not, but lie." Paul made similar statements in Romans: "For he is not a Jew who is one outwardly, nor is circumcision that which is outward in the flesh. But he is a Jew who is one inwardly; and circumcision is that which is of the heart, by the Spirit, not by the letter, and his praise is not from men, but from God" (Rom. 2:28–29). Being culturally and racially Jewish had no salvific value for these opponents of the gospel. Upholding the ceremonial law didn't change the fact that they had rejected Christ. They were physical descendants of Abraham, but they were not God's people. As Paul succinctly puts it, "They are not all Israel who are descended from Israel" (Rom. 9:6).

Incredibly, Christ promises the Philadelphian church, "I will make them come and bow down at your feet, and make them know that I have loved you" (Rev. 3:9). That's the posture of a humbled and defeated enemy, and that's precisely what this promise is indicating. Isaiah repeatedly prophesies of a similar humiliation for God's enemies in the future messianic kingdom:

> "The products of Egypt and the merchandise of Cush
> And the Sabeans, men of stature,
> Will come over to you and will be yours;

They will walk behind you, they will come over in chains
And will bow down to you;
They will make supplication to you:
'Surely, God is with you, and there is none else,
No other God.'"
(ISA. 45:14)

"Kings will be your guardians,
And their princesses your nurses.
They will bow down to you with their faces to the earth
And lick the dust of your feet;
And you will know that I am the LORD;
Those who hopefully wait for Me will not be put to shame."
(ISA. 49:23)

"The sons of those who afflicted you will come bowing
    to you,
And all those who despised you will bow themselves at
    the soles of your feet;
And they will call you the city of the LORD,
The Zion of the Holy One of Israel."
(ISA. 60:14)

This is not just a promise that the Philadelphian Christians will prevail over their persecutors. It's a promise that some of those same persecutors will *come to salvation through faith in the Christ they once opposed*. They will be humbled before the church because they will understand that God's love is not limited to Israel. They will recognize that there is no other name by which they can be saved, and they will put their trust in Christ alone. This is a foretaste of the day when "all Israel will be saved" (Rom. 11:26). Zechariah tells us the Lord will "pour out on the house of David and on the inhabitants of Jerusalem, the Spirit of grace and of supplication, so that they will look on Me whom they have pierced; and they will mourn for Him, as one mourns for an only son, and they will weep bitterly over Him like the bitter weeping over a firstborn" (Zech. 12:10). The believers in Philadelphia could endure the scorn of the Jews, knowing that in a short time, some of their persecutors would be fellow believers in the Lord.

DELIVERANCE FOR THE WHOLE CHURCH

Christ delivers a third promise in His letter to Philadelphia. He says, "Because you have kept the word of My perseverance, I also will keep you from the hour of testing, that hour which is about to come upon the whole world, to test those who dwell on the earth. I am coming quickly" (Rev. 3:10–11). If this promise refers to an actual historical event, we don't know what it was. It's entirely possible that there was a wave of persecution or a natural disaster that occurred in the area, or some other catastrophe during which the Lord protected and preserved this church. But if this promise was for a specific hour of testing that faced the church at Philadelphia, we don't know when it was or what happened.

However, the language Christ uses here is vast and sweeping, pointing to a fulfillment beyond just the believers in Philadelphia. Many believe this is the Holy Spirit giving us a look down through redemptive history to a time of severe judgment, that the Lord's words here refer to the rapture.

In 1 Corinthians 15:51–53, Paul describes that future event when Christ will take His church from earth to heaven: "Behold, I tell you a mystery; we will not all sleep, but we will all be changed, in a moment, in the twinkling of an eye, at the last trumpet; for the trumpet will sound, and the dead will be raised imperishable, and we will be changed. For this perishable must put on imperishable, and this mortal will have put on immortality." In the upper room, Christ told His disciples, "Do not let your heart be troubled; believe in God, believe also in Me. In My Father's house are many dwelling places; if it were not so, I would have told you; for I go to prepare a place for you. If I go and prepare a place for you, I will come again and receive you to Myself, that where I am, there you may be also. And you know the way where I am going" (John 14:1–4).

Both of those passages describe, not a judgment event, but Christ retrieving His people out of the world, catching them up into glory—the rapture (or catching away) of the saints. In 1 Thessalonians 4:13–18, Paul describes this event as an encouragement to those mourning the deaths of other believers:

> But we do not want you to be uninformed, brethren, about those who are asleep, so that you will not grieve as do the rest who have no hope. For if we believe that Jesus died and rose again, even so God will bring with Him those who have fallen asleep in Jesus. For this we say to you by the word of the Lord, that we who are alive and remain until the coming of the Lord, will not precede those who have fallen asleep. For the Lord Himself will descend from heaven with a shout, with the voice of the archangel and with the trumpet of God, and the dead in Christ will rise first. Then we who are alive and remain will be caught up together with them in the clouds to meet the Lord in the air, and so we shall always be with the Lord. Therefore comfort one another with these words.

While it's unmistakable in Scripture that the rapture will occur, believers are divided over its timing in relation to other eschatological events— specifically, the time of tribulation. In Matthew 24:21, Christ warns His disciples, "For then there will be a great tribulation, such as has not occurred since the beginning of the world until now, nor ever will." The tribulation is a seven-year period, marked by the reign of the Antichrist and a series of cataclysmic judgments poured out by God, including the seal, trumpet, and bowl judgments (Rev. 6–16). It is the period of eschatological history that immediately precedes the Lord's return to judge sinners with death and hell, and then establish His millennial kingdom on earth.

Regarding the timing of the rapture in relation to the tribulation, there are several long-standing ideas. Some believe in *posttribulationism*—that the church will endure the tribulation and be raptured from the world immediately prior to the Lord's return for the judgment of the world and to establish His earthly kingdom with the living believers. Others believe in *midtribulationism*—that the Lord will, in the middle of the tribulation, rapture His church before the fullness of God's wrath is poured out in the final three and a half years. There is also the *prewrath* view, which points to a rapture sometime after the midpoint of the tribulation but prior to God's final outpouring of wrath at the end of the tribulation. The other view, for which Revelation 3:10 serves as a critical support, is known as *pretribulationism*.

In this view, Christ's words in verse 10 are a promise that He will rescue His whole church "from the hour of testing, that hour which is about to come upon the whole world, to test those who dwell on the earth" (the tribulation). The pivotal phrase in the original Greek is *tēreō ek* ("keep from"). Pretribulationists see this as a promise that God will spare the church from His wrath, that He will keep them from it (see 1 Thess. 1:9–10). Proponents of the other views instead interpret this as a promise that God will preserve His church *through* the rapture—or at least portions of it. There are some compelling reasons to understand Revelation 3:10 from the pretribulationist perspective.

First of all, the only other time that Greek phrase *tēreō ek* appears in Scripture is in John 17:15. During His High Priestly Prayer, the Lord says, "I do not ask You to take them out of the world, but to keep them from the evil one." Christ did not pray for His people to merely *endure within the grasp of Satan's power*, but for them to be *kept out* of it altogether. In both instances, John is the author quoting directly from Christ. There is no compelling reason to read them with two different meanings.

Then there are the implications of interpreting this as a promise of preservation rather than removal. To begin with, Scripture tells us that believers during the tribulation will suffer and be killed for their faith (see Rev. 6:9–11; 7:9–14). In what sense, then, would the Lord be keeping His church from the time of testing if they are being slaughtered as well as subjected to the horrors of that period? If it is only a promise of protection from His own wrath—but not the wrath of Satan, hell's demons, the Antichrist, and the unrepentant world system—that doesn't seem like any comfort. Moreover, if the intent here is that He will simply preserve His church *through* the tribulation, how do His words apply to the believers at Philadelphia, who died long before it occurred?

The most acceptable understanding of Revelation 3:10 is as a gracious promise from the Lord to His faithful church—that for their perseverance in obedience to Him, they will be spared the fury of His temporal judgment poured out on the earth during the tribulation.

In that sense, His words in verse 11—"I am coming quickly"—are not meant as a warning of judgment, as they have been to other churches (2:5, 16, 25; 3:3). Instead, it is a hopeful look forward to the moment He will retrieve His own out of the world. And we should respond to that glorious hope by echoing John's sentiment at the end of Revelation: "Amen. Come, Lord Jesus" (22:20).

THE CROWN AND THE PILLAR

In the meantime, Christ warns His people to "hold fast what you have, so that no one will take your crown" (Rev. 3:11). "Hold fast to what you have" is a call to persevere. We've seen already that perseverance is the test of genuine faith and salvation (see Matt. 24:13;

1 John 2:19). But perseverance is not passive. In his letter to the Colossians, Paul explains how the Lord works through the faith of His people to hold them for eternity: "He has now reconciled you in His fleshly body through death, in order to present you before Him holy and blameless and beyond reproach—if indeed you continue in the faith firmly established and steadfast, and not moved away from the hope of the gospel that you have heard" (Col. 1:22–23). We must hold fast to Christ, even as He holds us.

The phrase "so that no one will take your crown" is not a threat that someone could steal a believer's salvation. Peter writes that our eternal inheritance is "imperishable and undefiled and will not fade away" (1 Peter 1:4). As Christ Himself said, "I give eternal life to them, and they will never perish; and no one will snatch them out of My hand. My Father, who has given them to Me, is greater than all; and no one is able to snatch them out of the Father's hand" (John 10:28–29). If this is a reference to the crown of life—the same one He promised to the church at Smyrna—there is nothing anyone could do to steal it. It could only be forfeited if the believer failed to persevere, proving that he was never truly saved in the first place (see 1 John 2:19).

On the other hand, it could be a warning to believers not to let others damage or diminish their eternal reward. As John urged his readers in his second epistle, "Watch yourselves, that you do not lose what we have accomplished, but that you may receive a full reward" (2 John 8). Perhaps this was a reminder to not let temporal concerns rob believers of the eternal reward for their faithfulness.

With eternal rewards in mind, Christ has some promises for those who overcome (see 1 John 5:4–5). He writes, "He who overcomes, I will make him a pillar in the temple of My God, and he will not go out from it anymore; and I will write on him the name of My God, and the name of the city of My God, the new Jerusalem, which comes down out of heaven from My God, and My new name" (Rev. 3:12).

What does it mean to be "a pillar in the temple of My God"? Pillars represent permanence and stability. To people whose homes and lives were frequently devastated by earthquakes, this was a promise of an unshakable, immovable place for them in the Lord's eternal sanctuary—a place "he will not go out from it anymore." They will perpetually live in the presence of the worship of God.

Yet there's more. Christ also promises, "I will write on him the name of My God." This is the equivalent of ownership and possession. For all eternity, we will bear the name of our Lord, which will mark us out as His precious children. Christ says He will also write on us "the name of the city of My God, the new Jerusalem, which comes down out of heaven from My God." Will we not only be designated as belonging to God, but also marked as eternal citizens of the New Jerusalem (see Rev. 21). Forever, we will enjoy all the rights and privileges of citizenship in God's eternal city.

Finally, Christ says He will write on us His "new name." Philippians 2:9 tells us, "God highly exalted Him, and bestowed on Him the name which is above every name." Christ's new name will reflect the perfection of our glorified relationship with Him, when "we will see Him just as He is" (1 John 3:2).

The Lord closes with the familiar reminder, "He who has an ear, let him hear what the Spirit says to the churches" (Rev. 3:13). In the case of His letter to Philadelphia, what we hear are the everlasting blessings and heavenly privileges the Lord will grant, not to those who have been perfect, but to those who have by His power been faithful.

9

The Lukewarm Church
LAODICEA

Who is the hardest person to reach with the gospel?

Is it the atheist? It's by no means easy to preach the gospel to someone who rejects the existence of God, along with His moral law, His sovereignty over His creation, and His authority to punish sin. Convincing the atheist that there is a God and that His law applies to him is definitely an uphill battle.

Perhaps it's the zealous religionist? Someone steeped in false teaching, trained in the apologetics of his or her faith, and prepared to debate and defend against the truth of the gospel. It's extremely difficult to penetrate decades of false religion and shine the light of God's truth into a heart devoted to spiritual darkness.

Or maybe the postmodern agnostic is the most difficult opponent of the gospel? With a skewed worldview that rejects the very notion of fixed, objective, authoritative, knowable truth, there is hardly enough common philosophical ground to even begin a conversation. Gospel opportunities are few and far between with such staunch opponents of absolute truth.

However, one type of unbeliever is harder to reach with the gospel than others. Worse than any outspoken, overt rejecter of God's Word is the self-righteous hypocrite who believes he doesn't need the gospel. He thinks that by his religion or morality he's on God's good side. Nothing is more spiritually deadly than false assurance of salvation. Nothing more rapidly inoculates a sinner to the Spirit's work through his conscience than the erroneous assumption that his sins have already been forgiven.

The church today is overrun with men and women who have never repented and believed savingly in the Lord, but are nonetheless convinced they are right with God and will not receive His judgment. Some of these people sit under the teaching of God's Word week after week, unmoved by its truth and unaware of the true condition of their hearts. They don't believe they remain lost in their sins. There's not much you could say or do to convince them of their need for the Savior.

As we'll see, that was the state of the church at Laodicea. Regarding the Lord's last letter to the churches in Revelation, John Stott wrote, "Perhaps none of the seven letters is more appropriate to the twentieth-century church than this. It describes vividly the respectable, sentimental, nominal, skin-deep religiosity which is so widespread among us today. Our Christianity is flabby and anemic. We appear to have taken a lukewarm bath of religion."[1]

The fact is, most of us drive past Laodicean churches every day—churches empty of saints but full of self-deceived sinners who are totally oblivious to the threat of God's judgment. These men and women have no hope of heaven. Their religious activity is a useless hypocrisy. They must be called to repent and believe. Christ's final letter is a powerful reminder that there is a vast and difficult mission field hiding in plain sight in church pews.

DON'T DRINK THE WATER

Founded more than two hundred and fifty years before the birth of Christ, Laodicea was the final city along the ancient postal route of Asia Minor. One of three cities in the Lycus River valley, along with Hierapolis (six miles to the north) and Colossae (ten miles to the east), it was located roughly forty-six miles southeast of Philadelphia. Founded by Antiochus II and named after his wife (whom he later divorced), Laodicea sat at the juncture of two primary trade routes. The road running north-south connected Pergamum to the Mediterranean Sea. The road stretching east-west reached from Ephesus to the interior regions of Asia Minor.

As a result, Laodicea was an important center of trade and commerce. The city specialized in the production of soft, black wool, used to make luxurious clothes and rugs. Historians indicate that Laodicea was a wealthy and prosperous city, and a hub for banking for the region. Unlike many of their neighboring communities, they declined Rome's help rebuilding after an earthquake in AD 60, preferring to cover the considerable cost themselves. The Roman historian Tacitus wrote, "One of the famous cities of Asia, Laodicea, was that same year overthrown by an earthquake, and, without any relief from us, recovered itself by its own resources."[2] The city was also a leader in ancient medicine. A medical school in the area had developed an eye salve that was sold throughout the Greco-Roman world. All three of those notable industries come up briefly in Christ's letter to the church.

For all the city's wealth and prominence, it had a significant and off-putting fault with its water supply. Nearby Hierapolis was known throughout the region for its natural hot springs. They remain a tourist attraction to this day. Colossae featured a perennially cold, natural stream. But Laodicea's nearest sources of water were either too polluted or inconsistent. To solve the problem, they constructed an underground aqueduct to deliver water into the city. However, traveling at least five miles through stone and clay pipes made the water filthy and unpleasant. It would have arrived to the city's central water tower tepid and dirty, smelling foul and tasting worse. From the ruins that remain, it's clear that the water contained significant amounts of calcium carbonate and other impurities. (Those ruins are located in the village of Eskihisar, near the city of Denizli in Turkey.)

We also know the city was home to a large Jewish population. In 62 BC, the governor Flaccus stopped the exporting of any gold out of the city. But the Jews always paid their Jerusalem shekel temple tax with gold, collected from all over the city and sent in one lump sum. When they attempted to defy his order and send the gold in secret, it was confiscated. The amount seized indicates there were thousands of Jewish families living in the city.

> [Flaccus] seized as contraband not less than twenty pounds weight in gold in the single district of which Laodicea was the capital. Calculated at the rate of a half-shekel for each man, this sum represents a population of more than eleven thousand adult freemen; for women, children, and slaves were exempted. It must be remembered however, that this is only the sum which the Roman officers succeeded in detecting and confiscating; and that therefore the whole Jewish population would probably be much larger than this partial estimate implies.[3]

As for the church in Laodicea, Scripture does not tell us when it was founded. It was likely part of the fruit of Paul's ministry in Ephesus (Acts 19:10), but it also could have been founded by believers in nearby Colossae. We know it wasn't founded by Paul himself, because he mentions the believers at Laodicea along with "all those who have not personally seen my face" in Colossians 2:1. Scripture suggests that Epaphras (Col. 1:7) and Archippus

(4:17) may have been leaders in the church at some point. What we do know is that there was a relationship between the churches of Colossae and Laodicea. At the end of his epistle to the Colossians, Paul writes, "Greet the brethren who are in Laodicea and also Nympha and the church that is in her house. When this letter is read among you, have it also read in the church of the Laodiceans; and you, for your part read my letter that is coming from Laodicea" (4:15–16). It's possible that the same false teaching that Paul addressed in his letter to the Colossians had also swept into the church at Laodicea with deadly influence.

Based on how the Lord describes Himself in His letter to this church, that seems likely.

DEBUNKING HERETICAL CHRISTOLOGY

In Revelation 3:14, the Lord identifies Himself as "The Amen, the faithful and true Witness, the Beginning of the creation of God." For the second time, Christ breaks away from His pattern of referring to the imagery from John's initial vision on Patmos (Rev. 1:9–20). In fact, there's no imagery here at all. He simply says He is "the Amen." The word *amen* is often used in Scripture to affirm the truthfulness of a statement. It's a verbal guarantee that what has been said is true. It carries the same essential meaning as the phrase "verily, verily" or "truly, truly" that appears before many of Christ's statements. *Verily* at the beginning of a statement affirms the truth of what is about to be said. An *amen* at the end seals the statement's veracity and certainty.

This is the only place in Scripture where the word serves as a title for Christ. It could be a reference to Isaiah 65:16, which twice refers to the "God of truth." There can be no doubt that title applies to our Lord as well, since He is the firm, faithful, unchangeable *Amen*.

But this isn't merely a comment about the truthfulness of the Lord and His promises. In 2 Corinthians 1:20, Paul writes, "For as many as are the promises of God, in Him they are yes; therefore also through Him is our Amen to the glory of God through us." Christ Himself is the fulfillment of all God's promises. Every promise of grace and blessing, every covenant of peace and forgiveness is validated in the person and work of Jesus Christ. The whole of the Old Testament points to Him, as He accomplishes and guarantees all of God's covenants with His people. He is God's Amen, the One who confirms all divine promises.

Christ also identifies Himself as "the faithful and true Witness" (Rev. 3:14). Not only does He validate what God has said and promised, but whatever He says is true, too. His words are always faithful and true. He is completely trustworthy and perfectly accurate. In the words of John 14:6, He is "the way, and *the truth*, and the life" (emphasis added).

When Christ speaks on behalf of God, His testimony is always true. Jesus is the Amen of God, the living verification and validation and confirmation of every promise God ever made, every plan God ever established, and every covenant He set. Beyond that, everything He says and does is sincere and true. At the outset of His letter to Laodicea, Christ establishes that truth itself is critical, and that He speaks with absolute accuracy and clarity regarding their spiritual condition.

There's a third phrase Christ uses to identify Himself in verse 14: He is "the Beginning of the creation of God." English translations cloud the meaning of the Lord's words here in misleading ambiguity. Many false teachers have attempted to use this verse to deny Christ's deity, asserting that He is simply a created being like the rest of us. That perverted Christology is fundamental to most modern cults and false religions. It is an ancient lie that traces back to the earliest days of the church. In fact, Paul wrote his epistle to the Colossians to protect them from succumbing to a similar strain of heresy. Regarding Christ's deity, the apostle wrote,

He is the image of the invisible God, the firstborn of
all creation. For by Him all things were created, both in
the heavens and on earth, visible and invisible, whether
thrones or dominions or rulers or authorities—all things
have been created through Him and for Him. He is
before all things, and in Him all things hold together.
He is also the head of the body, the church; and He is
the beginning, the firstborn from the dead, so that He
Himself will come to have first place in everything. For
it was the Father's good pleasure for all the fullness to
dwell in Him.

(COL. 1:15–19)

The word translated as "firstborn" in Colossians 1:15 is *prōtotokos*.
It does not signify mere chronology, but preeminence and supremacy. In the same way, the Greek word translated in Revelation 3:14
as "Beginning" (*archē*) is not ambiguously identifying Christ as part
of the creation, but rather as its *source*. John affirmed this truth in his
gospel: "All things came into being through Him, and apart from
Him nothing came into being that has come into being" (John 1:3;
see also Heb. 1:2). Christ is not another created being; He is the
Creator, the Author of all physical and spiritual life.

The same false teaching that threatened the Colossian church
had likely made its way to Laodicea. That heretical view of Christ
might have been the cause of the Laodicean church's apostasy and
spiritual decay. As an unregenerate church, they didn't believe that
Christ was the *archē*, the Initiator and Originator of life and all that
exists. They denied that He was the uncreated source of creation.
They didn't believe that He was "the Alpha and the Omega" (Rev.
1:8), the supreme sovereign Creator and Consummator of all things.

Like many unregenerate churches, the Laodiceans had a warped
view of Christ. Their heresy was no different from that of the Mor-
mon church, the Jehovah's Witnesses, or any of the liberal churches

today that reject Scripture and the deity of Christ. From the outset, Christ's letter to the Laodiceans demonstrates that the church had erred disastrously in Christology, and their blasphemous beliefs were a grave offense to the Lord. To expose and combat their heresy, He delivers a powerful theological statement that affirms His deity and authority, even over this apostate, unregenerate church: He is the Lord who created everything, the faithful and true Witness to the Word of God, and the One in whom all God's spiritual promises are fulfilled. And He demands to be worshiped as such.

The letter to the church at Laodicea powerfully illustrates the deadly and horrifying spiritual effects of perverting the truth concerning the person and work of Christ.

TRIGGERING THE DIVINE GAG REFLEX

Laodicea has the grim distinction of being the only church to which Christ says nothing good at all. There are no redeeming features to be declared about anyone in this congregation. Apparently, there was no wheat whatsoever, only tares. The Lord delivers nothing but unsparing condemnation for this unregenerate church. He says, "I know your deeds, that you are neither cold nor hot; I wish that you were cold or hot. So because you are lukewarm, and neither hot nor cold, I will spit you out of My mouth" (Rev. 3:15–16). It's a blunt and picturesque statement. In effect, He says, "I know you. I know what you are. You are lukewarm. You make Me want to vomit."

This would have been a particularly vivid condemnation for the citizens of Laodicea. Their water wasn't hot like it was in Hierapolis. It wasn't cold and clear like the stream that fed into Colossae. Instead, the water in Laodicea was mucky, toxic, and tepid. Flowing through miles of filthy clay and stone pipes, it became contaminated and disgusting, unable to quench thirst or restore strength. Quite literally, it was nauseating. With imagery that would have been immediately familiar to every resident of Laodicea, the Lord delivered a stunning rebuke for the church there: you make Me sick.

Christ says, "I wish you were cold or hot" (v. 15). Spiritually hot people are alive and fervent in their love for the Lord. They exhibit the transforming work of the Spirit, and a passion for reaching the lost with the gospel. On the other hand, spiritually cold people openly reject the truth of God's Word and salvation through His Son. They are spiritually dull and dead, with no interest in Christ or His church.

The lukewarm Laodiceans landed squarely in the middle. They couldn't be hot because they were still unregenerate. But they didn't qualify as cold either, because they had not publicly rejected the truth. Instead, they were pious hypocrites, claiming to love the Lord while privately holding to a false Christ and a false gospel. They maintained an outward show of faith and devotion to the Lord, but like the Pharisees, theirs was a self-satisfied, self-righteous religion. In his second letter to Timothy, Paul described the lukewarm as those "holding to a form of godliness, although they have denied its power" (2 Tim. 3:5). The Lord warned His disciples of the horrifying future that awaits such spiritual pretenders: "Many will say to Me on that day, 'Lord, Lord, did we not prophesy in Your name, and in Your name cast out demons, and in Your name perform many miracles?' And then I will declare to them, 'I never knew you; depart from Me, you who practice lawlessness'" (Matt. 7:22–23).

Such hypocritical churches have always existed throughout church history, filled with unconverted and unrepentant people, proclaiming all sorts of false doctrines and erroneous opinions about Christ. They *nauseate* the Lord. That's a more visceral reaction than we've seen from Christ as He confronts the other churches of Asia Minor. He was disappointed with the Ephesian church that had abandoned its first love. His anger burned against the churches that had compromised with the world and invited corruption into their midst. But the lukewarm Laodicean church was disgusting. Christ wanted to spit them out of His mouth. Their failure to be hot or cold was a rank and revolting offense to the Lord of heaven.

Either extreme would have been preferable to the Lord. Even openly cold hearts would have been a more honest reflection of their true spiritual state—and it would have left them open to feeling the sting of sin's guilt. Instead, they lulled themselves into spiritual self-satisfaction, unaware that their heresy and hypocrisy had dulled their ability to assess their own spiritual condition accurately.

Christ describes the depth of their self-deception in His letter: "You say, 'I am rich, and have become wealthy, and have need of nothing,' and you do not know that you are wretched and miserable and poor and blind and naked" (Rev. 3:17). The Lord tells them they are absolutely ignorant of their true spiritual condition. The same is true of all unbelievers who come together in a "church"; they're in no position to assess the state of their hearts. They are collectively blinded to spiritual reality.

Laodicea was famous for its material wealth. It seems that the church's own identity was bound up not just in the false security of those material riches, but also in their supposed spiritual wealth. But that was a baseless fiction. Their spiritual self-assurance might be an indication of another strain of false teaching that had poisoned the Laodicean church. In addition to their blasphemous view of Christ, they, like some in the Colossian assembly, may have been influenced by an early form of Gnosticism. The Gnostics believed they had obtained a kind of secret, elevated knowledge. Their supposedly transcendent knowledge set them apart from other unsophisticated believers. That's the kind of spiritual pride Christ described in His letter to Laodicea: "I am rich, and have become wealthy, and have need of nothing" (v. 17).

Spiritually speaking, that is the worst state a person can be in. It would be far better to be an atheist or completely ignorant of the church and the gospel. Truly, *anything* would be better than the Laodicean's self-righteous hypocrisy. Their apostasy was all-encompassing. They knew the truth about Christ but denied His deity; they knew the truth about God but worshiped a god of their own design. Such smug spiritual self-confidence characterizes whole denominations today. It likewise characterizes many supposedly Christian institutions, universities, and seminaries. They believe they are spiritually rich and that their knowledge sets them above and apart from the *hoi polloi*, but they have no appreciation for how nauseating they are to the Lord they profess.

That's true of any church or institution dominated by self-deceived nonbelievers. It's a sickening condition of thinking you're spiritually rich when you're bankrupt, of thinking you're beautiful when you're ugly, of imagining you're to be envied when you're utterly pitiable, of believing you see everything clearly when you're lost and blind, of believing you're draped in spiritual finery when you're filthy and naked. That was the situation for the Laodiceans. The Lord confronted them bluntly with the reality of their situation: "You do not know that you are wretched and miserable and poor and blind and naked" (v. 17).

Believers need to show mercy to the unbelieving world. We need to reach out whenever and wherever possible with the truth of the gospel. But we must also reach out just as vigorously to those in the midst of the church who are lost in self-deception and hypocrisy. Blinded to their desperate need for the Savior, these men and women need to be regularly confronted with the truth of the Word of God, the gospel of grace, and of the Lord Jesus Christ. We must pray that divine grace and mercy, repentance and faith, are still available to them.

That was the Lord's message to the apostate church at Laodicea.

A GRACIOUS OFFER TO AN APOSTATE CHURCH

As a remedy to their wretched spiritual state, Christ says, "I advise you to buy from Me gold refined by fire so that you may become rich, and white garments so that you may clothe yourself, and that the shame of your nakedness will not be revealed; and eye salve to anoint your eyes so that you may see" (Rev. 3:18). Christ offers grace to these hypocrites. He could have judged them on the spot, but He withholds their destruction and calls them to repent.

His words emphasize the Laodiceans' false sense of security, as He compares His offer of salvation to the emptiness of their supposed wealth. As we noted earlier, the city was known for its financial prosperity, its wool industry, and the production of eye salve. In this one verse, the Lord upends that local pride and illustrates just how spiritually poor, blind, and destitute they were without Him.

Of course, their money could not buy what they needed from the Lord. No amount of money could redeem and save their souls. Instead, Christ's words emphasized the futility of their material riches. Their vast wealth, significant as it was, could not do them any lasting spiritual good. His advice to "buy from Me" is an echo of God's words through the prophet Isaiah: "Ho! Every one who thirsts, come to the waters; and you who have no money come, buy and eat. Come, buy wine and milk without money and without cost" (Isa. 55:1). Christ's righteousness is not for sale to sinners; the price has already been paid.

The Lord directed the unredeemed church at Laodicea to buy three items, all symbolizing the redemption they so desperately needed. The first was "gold refined by fire so that you may become rich" (Rev. 3:18). The people of Laodicea would have been familiar enough with gold to understand the great value of what Christ was offering here. This spiritual gold had been refined and purged of impurities. It was perfect and priceless, especially when compared to the physical gold they so highly prized. Peter described true saving faith as "more precious than gold which is perishable, even though tested by fire" (1 Peter 1:7). The Laodiceans trusted in their vast wealth. Christ offered them the true spiritual riches of salvation and a right relationship with Him.

He also instructed them to buy, "white garments so that you may clothe yourself, and that the shame of your nakedness will not be revealed" (Rev. 3:18). Throughout these letters to the churches of Asia Minor, Christ has mentioned these white robes. The imagery shows up again later in the book of Revelation. As noted previously, when speaking of the saints in glory, the white robes may depict their cleansed and purified works of obedience (see 3:4–5; 19:8). Here the white robe represents the righteousness of Christ imputed to believers (see 7:13–14). The famous black wool clothes that came from Laodicea were symbolic of the sin that covered the nakedness of the Laodicean hypocrites. The garments they required were the ones Isaiah described: "I will rejoice greatly in the LORD, my soul will exult in my God; for He has clothed me with garments of salvation, He has wrapped me with a robe of righteousness" (Isa. 61:10). Their self-righteousness was nothing more than filthy rags (Isa. 64:6). They needed to be cloaked in the righteousness of Christ (2 Cor. 5:21).

Finally, the Lord told the Laodiceans to buy from Him "eye salve to anoint your eyes so that you may see" (Rev. 3:18). The eye salve that the Laodiceans produced and sold was no miracle cure. At best, it was able to soothe irritated eyes. That's a stark contrast to the salve Christ offers unrepentant sinners—one that opens their spiritual eyes to His truth. In 2 Corinthians 4:4, Paul writes that "the god of this world has blinded the minds of the unbelieving so that they might not see the light of the gospel of the glory of Christ." Unredeemed sinners are lost in their spiritual blindness, unaware of their bondage to Satan and unable to appreciate the light of the gospel. They need Christ to "open their eyes so that they may turn from darkness to light and from the dominion of Satan to God, that they may receive forgiveness of sins" (Acts 26:18). The false church at Laodicea had been blinded by heresy and hypocrisy. They needed the Lord to open their eyes and shine the light of His truth into their hearts.

Though Christ's words here are a call to unbelievers, they're also a powerful reminder to the true church as well. Salvation is the gold that makes us spiritually rich in faith. It is the white robe that covers our sinful nakedness with the righteousness of God through Christ. It is the eye salve that gives us the knowledge of God's illuminating grace and an understanding of His truth. This is a magnificent image of the threefold blessings of salvation, the treasure the Lord freely pours out on His people.

DIVINE LOVE FOR THE LOST

Christ's words in Revelation 3:19 have led some to believe that the church at Laodicea was not entirely apostate, that there were some in the congregation who were saved. The Lord says, "Those whom I love, I reprove and discipline; therefore be zealous and repent." While it might initially sound like He is talking to Christians, the context won't allow for that interpretation, as verses 18 and 20 do not equivocate on the spiritual condition of the unregenerate audience.

We must be careful not to sequester God's love to His elect alone. Passages like Psalm 145:8–9, Matthew 5:44–48, and Mark 10:21 make it clear that the Lord does love even the world of unrepentant, reprobate sinners with a love of true compassion. It's not the divine love spoken of in 1 John 4:9–11 or Romans 5:8 that sovereignly secures redemption for its object, but it is an unfeigned, kindhearted tenderness. Here in the letter to Laodicea, Christ explains that His love for the world includes the way He reproves and disciplines their sin. "Reprove" is another way to say He exposes and convicts them of their sin. Describing the work of the Holy Spirit through the consciences of sinful men, Christ said, "And He, when He comes, will convict the world concerning sin and righteousness and judgment" (John 16:8). God loves the world by exposing its sin and by punishing it. The word translated in Revelation 3:19 as "discipline" is used twice in Luke 23, where it is translated as "punish," describing Christ's torture at the hands of Pilate. In 2 Timothy 2:25, it is used to refer to God's conviction of unbelievers. The point is that God's love for sinners begins with the unmasking of our wretchedness. If we've been saved by grace through faith in Christ, it's because the Lord first impressed upon us the guilt of our sin and the weight of His wrath. His love for each of us began with reproof and discipline.

There's a note of tenderness in these words, as there is in the whole letter. In spite of their heresy and hypocrisy, the Lord has a tender affection for the people of Laodicea. He doesn't love them with an *agape* kind of love. Instead, it's *phileo*—a divine affection apart from a right spiritual relationship. He is compassionately calling on these unregenerate Laodiceans to come to saving faith in Him and avoid His wrath. The Lord made a similar statement to Israel in Ezekiel 33:11: "'As I live!' declares the Lord GOD, 'I take no pleasure in the death of the wicked, but rather that the wicked turn from his way and live. Turn back, turn back from your evil ways! Why then will you die, O house of Israel?'"

Moreover, He shows them the path to a right relationship with Him, urging them to "be zealous and repent" (Rev. 3:19). The gospel message of Christ always involves repentance (Matt. 4:17). Sinners must mourn over their sin and hunger for the righteousness that only Christ can provide. In 2 Corinthians 7:10, Paul explained mere regret and true repentance: "For the sorrow that is according to the will of God produces a repentance without regret, leading to salvation, but the sorrow of the world produces death." It's important to understand that repentance is not a meritorious act. Rather, it is a vital step in God's saving work, what Acts 11:18 calls "the repentance that leads to life."

In his *Studies in the Sermon on the Mount*, D. Martyn Lloyd-Jones gives us this powerful insight into the nature of true repentance:

Repentance means that you realize that you are a guilty, vile sinner in the presence of God, that you deserve the wrath and punishment of God, that you are hell-bound. It means that you begin to realize that this thing called sin is in you, that you long to get rid of it, and that you turn your back on it in every shape and form. You renounce the world whatever the cost, the world in its mind and outlook as well as its practice, and you deny yourself, and take up the cross and go after Christ.[4]

Paul describes the urgency of Christ's call to repent in Acts 17:30–31: "Therefore having overlooked the times of ignorance, God is now declaring to men that all people everywhere should repent, because He has fixed a day in which He will judge the world in righteousness through a Man who He has appointed, having furnished proof to all men by raising Him from the dead." Christ's love for the unbelieving world is most evident in His patience and long-suffering, as He mercifully grants sinners time to repent and believe.

But the Lord's tenderness for the apostate Laodiceans is not limited to His call to repent. In verse 20, He delivers this very personal promise: "Behold, I stand at the door and knock; if anyone hears My voice and opens the door, I will come in to him and will dine with him, and he with Me." This invitation is one of the most familiar in all of Scripture, but also one of the most misunderstood.

Revelation 3:20 is frequently deployed by evangelists and preachers as a personal, urgent plea from the Lord. It's explained as a promise that Christ merely waits on the doorstep of every sinner's heart, eager to be granted access. It often appears in tandem with the similarly unbiblical sentiment of "asking Jesus into your heart." Both clichés expose the man-centered view of salvation that confuses and corrupts much of the church today—one that veers sharply away from Paul's words in Ephesians 2:

And you were dead in your trespasses and sins, in which
you formerly walked according to the course of this
world, according to the prince of the power of the air, of
the spirit that is now working in the sons of disobedience. Among them we too all formerly lived in the lusts
of our flesh, indulging the desires of the flesh and of the
mind, and were by nature children of wrath, even as the
rest. But God, being rich in mercy, because of His great
love with which He loved us, even when we were dead
in our transgressions, made us alive together with Christ
(by grace you have been saved), and raised us up with
Him, and seated us with Him in the heavenly places in
Christ Jesus, so that in the ages to come He might show
the surpassing riches of His grace in kindness toward
us in Christ Jesus. For by grace you have been saved
through faith; and that not of yourselves, it is the gift of
God; not as a result of works, so that no one may boast.
(vv. 1–9)

Despite its frequent misapplication, Revelation 3:20 is not a
general statement about Christ's knocking on the heart's door of
sinners, nor is it an accurate picture of His call to repent. The fact
is, the door Christ refers to here was a specific door, not the meta-
phorical door of every human heart. This is a specific invitation to
the church at Laodicea and others like it. Christ was not in that
church, further proof that, unlike the church at Sardis, there were
no believers in the Laodicean congregation at all. In verse 20, He
promised to come and bring the reality of true salvation into that
apostate group if even some would respond to His call to repent
and receive Him!

Today, the Lord is similarly shut out of countless churches that
claim His name, but regularly dishonor Him. Whether they're dead
liberal churches, churches with a fake gospel, or cults, they have no

interest in the biblical Christ or the salvation He offers. And just as with the church at Laodicea, it takes the true expression of repentance and faith to open the door to Christ's presence and influence.

But it's not just a presence in the church as a minimal blessing that He promises here. He says, "I will come in to him and will dine with him, and he with Me" (v. 20). A shared meal was a symbol of unity, fellowship, and intimacy. As we've already seen, believers will one day celebrate the marriage supper of the Lamb with Christ (Rev. 19:9). We look forward to eternal intimacy with our Lord and Savior in heaven. Through the indwelling of the Holy Spirit, we get a foretaste of that fellowship here on earth. It was that blessed communion that Christ promised to anyone in the Laodicean church who would repent and believe.

The word translated as "dine" refers to the evening meal, the final event of the day. This is the Lord's final plea to this church. He's still outside the church, waiting in the waning hours before the night of His judgment falls and it is everlastingly too late for the Laodiceans to repent.

Again, there is boundless grace in the Lord's kind forbearance with sinners. He faithfully pleads with them to repent as He extends grace and continues to withhold His wrath against the world and its wickedness. Christ's letter to the church at Laodicea is a grim reminder of the cost of heresy and hypocrisy, but it also offers encouragement about the Lord's love for sinners and His desire to bring them to salvation.

The Lord closes His letter to the Laodicean church with a word for to all believers. To His overcomers (see 1 John 5:4–5), the Lord promises, "He who overcomes, I will grant to him to sit down with Me on My throne, as I also overcame and sat down with My Father on His throne" (Rev. 3:21). This is the pinnacle of Christ's promised blessings for believers who faithfully persevere, which we are unable to fully comprehend. Paul delivered a similar promise in 2 Timothy 2:12: "If we endure, we will also reign with Him." Christ promises not only immediate fellowship to believers, but also to grant us to reign by His side for eternity. This is a picture of perfect intimacy in glorious authority. It's the supreme elevation of redeemed humanity and a vivid reminder that we do not receive a minimal salvation in Christ, but that we are grafted into God's family and granted all the privileges of sonship in His eternal kingdom.

The Lord ends His letter with the familiar reminder: "He who has an ear, let him hear what the Spirit says to the churches" (Rev. 3:22). In the case of the letter to the church at Laodicea, that's a warning to the apostates, to the Christ-deniers, to the liberals, and to the cultists who think they're elevated, scholarly, and enlightened above and beyond the plain testimony of Scripture. Christ confronts their spiritual blindness and poverty head on, and asserts His deity and authority without apology. He demolishes their self-righteous façades and forces them to see their apostasy and hypocrisy for the sinful offense it truly is. He extends grace to those who repent and embrace Him as Lord and Savior.

We must do the same while there is still time.

10

*The Need for a
New Reformation*

Christians frequently talk about the need for reformation in the church. But what would a truly biblical revival of the body of Christ look like? Not just a brief stirring of Christian hearts in a local setting, but a global spiritual revival of the whole church? What would it mean to have a new reformation today? What would change? And what needs to happen to trigger such a revival?

To begin with, the church would have to pursue obedience to the Lord's command to be holy as He is holy (1 Peter 1:16). God's people need to bring an end to foolish dalliances with worldliness and get serious about dealing with the sin in their midst. That's the kind of reformation the Lord calls for—one that emphasizes a committed love for Christ, the exclusion of worldly compromise, the consistent confrontation of sin, and a serious plea for sound theology and personal holiness.

But the reformation the church desperately needs isn't the product of some new strategy or emphasis. Believers don't need someone to blaze a new methodological trail or cast an exciting new vision for the church to match the perspectives of the twenty-first century.

The fact is the church isn't facing unique problems that demand clever new solutions. Satan's strategies have not changed, and "we are not ignorant of his schemes" (2 Cor. 2:11). He assaults the church today in the same ways he did in the first century. If anything, what has changed is the church's willingness to compromise with the world and accommodate false teaching. Rather than engaging in spiritual warfare against satanic lies and anti-Christian ideologies (2 Cor. 10:4), too many churches have declared an unbiblical truce with the world and stopped fighting for God's truth altogether.

Innovative church models and unorthodox evangelistic strategies won't solve the problems we're facing. New methods for the church that aren't tethered to biblical wisdom or the pursuit of holiness are not the solution; they're how we got here in the first place. More of the same won't solve the problem.

Rather, God's people need to recover and reaffirm the historical, theological principles behind the life transformations that invite true reformation in the first place. All the issues that ail and impair the church today could be dealt with by a renewed emphasis on the very same five *solas* of the Protestant Reformation in the sixteenth century.

SOLA SCRIPTURA

As mentioned in chapter 1, absolute trust in Scripture alone as the ultimate and sufficient authority in the church is known as the formal principle of the Reformation. It was the necessary foundation for all other key Reformation doctrines, and it was the first and primary point of departure from the corrupting influence of the Catholic Church. Others before Martin Luther had complained about Rome's abuses and false doctrine, but the Reformation was born out of Luther's relentless appeals to the authority of Scripture.

Historically, that is the pattern with revival. Every great movement of God in the world is launched by the recovery of Scripture.

It was the cause of a great spiritual awakening among the people of Israel after their exile. In Nehemiah 8, Ezra calls for the book of the Law and reads it before the people, prompting repentance and a dramatic revival throughout Jerusalem. Israel's history was marked by patterns of rebellion and revival, with their repentance always a product of remembering and returning to God's Word.

The Reformation was a result of a similar renewed commitment to the singular authority of God's Word in His church. And bound up in that recognition of the Bible's authority was an implicit affirmation of its sufficiency. The Bible is not only the inspired, authoritative Word of God, but also sufficient to meet the needs of God's people—"for teaching, for reproof, for correction, for training in righteousness; so that the man of God may be adequate, *equipped for every good work*" (2 Tim. 3:16–17, emphasis added). Scripture is sufficient for the salvation of the elect and the sanctification of the redeemed. It edifies the saints and informs their hope of eternity. It abundantly supplies instruction, correction, encouragement, and assurance to God's people.

Scripture speaks to its own authority and sufficiency in Revelation 22:18–19, sternly warning anyone who would presume to add to or take away from the Word of God.

> I testify to everyone who hears the words of the prophecy of this book: if anyone adds to them, God will add to him the plagues which are written in this book; and if anyone takes away from the words of the book of this prophecy, God will take away his part from the tree of life and from the holy city, which are written in this book.

As the singular, sufficient, and final authority over the church, God's Word is not subject to addition, subtraction, or editorial revision.

Imagine the impact that a renewed commitment to Scripture's

authority and sufficiency would have in churches today. To begin with, it would strike a massive blow against the educated heretics who have believed the lies of critical academics. It would silence the men and women who presume to sit in judgment of God's Word, dismissing it as nothing more than literature, fables, and allegory to be interpreted by personal whim and social concerns. And it would bring an end to the church's interest in theological novelty and innovation, and restore the emphasis to biblical fidelity, sound doctrine, and faithful exposition.

An emphasis on *sola Scriptura* would also stifle the deceptions of charlatans who base their ministries on supposed fresh revelation and personal impressions from the Lord. Superstitions about private messages from God have plagued the church in almost every generation of church history. Virtually every sub-Christian cult has been founded by someone claiming to have heard directly from God. Almost no idea has left more destruction in its wake. But belief in ongoing revelation has become a hallmark of the charismatic movement, and the far reach of its influence has sown into the church an appetite for fresh words from God, creating a global epidemic of professing Christians who believe the Bible isn't enough.

I occasionally watch the faith healers and prosperity preachers on television, and I've noticed a consistent trend in their teaching. Most of these men and women teach almost exclusively in the first person. They stomp back and forth across the stage explaining how "The Lord told me this . . ." and "He showed me that . . . ," while the Bible stays parked on the podium, useful only as a reference tool to back up their "fresh words from heaven." That whole approach to teaching is antibiblical, and it has created a false Christianity based on personal intuition and subjective insight.

Perhaps the most recent examples to capture the attention of the church are the bestselling devotionals presented as collections of personal insights and messages received from God, which have sold in the tens of millions. One of them opens with this introduction:

I began to wonder if I, too, could receive messages during my times of communing with God. I had been writing in prayer journals for years, but that was one-way communication: I did all the talking. I knew that God communicated with me through the Bible, but I yearned for more. Increasingly, I wanted to hear what God had to say to me personally on a given day. I decided to listen to God with pen in hand, writing down whatever I believed He was saying.[1]

While these wildly popular books do not necessarily advocate for the charismatic movement, they represent the worst of its doctrinal error. More deceitful than the ridiculous promises of healing and prosperity, and worse than the nonsensical gibberish of tongues, these books and others of the same genre export the lie of the charismatics: that God is just waiting to give to almost anyone new revelation beyond Scripture. This notion that God is still speaking to people through dreams, mental impressions, gut feelings, and audible voices is an implicit denial of the final authority and complete sufficiency of Scripture.

And that trend is not isolated to those under the influence of the charismatic movement or mystical nonsense. Any approach to "spiritual formation" that encourages Christians to listen for the voice of God inside their heads or anywhere else outside of Scripture undermines the authority, sufficiency, and God-breathed uniqueness of the written Word. An essential aspect of true spiritual maturity is "learn[ing] not to exceed what is written" (1 Cor. 4:6). Any practice that encourages believers to look inward for answers rather than to God and His Word is nothing more than repackaged Eastern mysticism in the guise of devotion to the Lord. In spite of the biblical language it invokes, it eagerly substitutes subjective impressions and personal feelings for biblical truth.

Other professing believers take a more circuitous approach

to undercutting the authority and sufficiency of God's Word by attempting to blend the truth of Scripture with worldly wisdom. Throughout much of the 1980s and '90s, psychology exerted a dominant force in the church. Pastors and church leaders abdicated their counseling duties, giving way to professionals with little (if any) biblical training. As I explained at the time in a book titled *Our Sufficiency in Christ*, "Too many have bought the lie that a crucial realm of wisdom exists outside Scripture and one's relationship to Jesus Christ, and that some idea or technique from that extrabiblical realm holds the real key to helping people with their deep problems."[2] That trend continues unabated.

We see the same assault on the authority of Scripture in the debate over the Genesis account of creation. Rather than accept the clarity of a literal translation of Genesis 1, many in the church perform all sorts of interpretive gymnastics to accommodate the world's conclusions about the universe's origins. Under the weight of so-called science, which cannot explain the massive miracle of creation, they reject the clear and simple reading of the text in favor of theories rooted in skepticism and unbelief. And they hobble the authority and sufficiency of Scripture by declaring its opening pages to be nothing more than a fable or a literary device. If Genesis can't be trusted, why should any other part of the Bible receive our absolute trust?

It's staggering how many false doctrines and erroneous practices in the church today are the direct result of compromising the authority and sufficiency of Scripture. A renewed commitment to *sola Scriptura* would silence those purporting to speak for God, and those sitting in judgment of what He has said. It would sweep aside the dream journals and fictional tales masquerading as divine revelation. And it would guard the church from the influence of those determined to mix biblical truth with worldly error. A renewed commitment to the authority, sufficiency, and clarity of Scripture is the starting place to purge the church of many of its most per-

The Need for a New Reformation

nicious impurities, and provide significant protection from Satan's corrupting influence.

SOLA FIDE

Justification by faith alone is the heart of the gospel. To reject *sola fide*, whether consciously or unconsciously, introduces a requirement of works that negates salvation. Good works play no part in delivering the sinner from the penalty sin deserves. In the apostle Paul's great treatise on the nature of justification, he explained that the sinner's only hope of salvation is found not in his own righteous deeds, but in the righteousness that comes by faith alone:

> But to the one who does not work, but believes in Him who justifies the ungodly, his faith is credited as righteousness, just as David also speaks of the blessing on the man to whom God credits righteousness apart from works: "Blessed are those whose lawless deeds have been forgiven, and whose sins have been covered. Blessed is the man whose sin the Lord will not take into account."
> (ROM. 4:5–8)

Faith alone is the means by which anyone has ever been made right with God. Israel's sacrificial system had no capacity to save sinners. Through the prophet Isaiah, the Lord told His people, "I take no pleasure in the blood of bulls, lambs or goats." Faith was always the basis of God's redemptive plan. Scripture is clear that Israel's patriarch Abraham was not saved by his piety, but because "he believed in the LORD; and He reckoned it to him as righteousness" (Gen. 15:6). The New Testament authors repeatedly quote that verse in defense of justification by faith alone (see Rom. 4:9; Gal. 3:6; James 2:23). Good works did not save Abraham, and they can't save anyone else. Moreover, Paul warned the Galatians, "If any man is preaching to you a gospel contrary to what you received, he is to be accursed!" (Gal. 1:9). The false gospel of works is the damnable heresy Paul was referring to.

The Roman Catholic Church pays lip service to the importance of faith, but Rome's dogma is built on a system of works-righteousness and meritorious rituals. In fact, the common thread shared by all false religions throughout history is the consistent focus on the justifying merit of human achievement. "But if [salvation] is by grace," Paul explains, "it is no longer on the basis of works, otherwise grace is no longer grace" (Rom. 11:6). Only biblical Christianity teaches that the justification of the sinner is an exclusively divine accomplishment, by faith alone.

However, as noted in chapter 1, fewer than half of all Protestants in America today believe that salvation comes by faith alone. They have been bewitched by a variety of false gospels and false assumptions. That flagging commitment to *sola fide* undergirds two of the errors corrupting the church today: ecumenism and easy-believism.

For too long, professing believers have searched for spiritual common ground between the evangelical church and proponents of corrupt false gospels. The blithe hope of co-laboring together with Catholics, Mormons, and others for the sake of moral reform or political advantages ignores the fact that *those religions don't preach the same gospel*. Others partner with unbelievers for the sake of social justice or the preservation of Judeo-Christian values. While such ecumenical pursuits don't in and of themselves necessarily constitute a corruption or compromise of the gospel, those who engage in them must be willing to call out the false and deceitful teachings of those with whom they are allied. To remain silent is to blur crucial doctrinal lines that delineate the true church from the false. Unfortunately, evangelicals who make ecumenical partnerships for the sake of gaining political influence do routinely mute essential gospel truths in order to avoid offense for the sake of preserving the coalition they have formed. Such silence is sin.

God's people must face the pointed words of Paul in 2 Corinthians 6:14–16: "Do not be bound together with unbelievers; for what partnership have righteousness and lawlessness, or what fellowship has light with darkness? Or what harmony has Christ with Belial, or what has a believer in common with an unbeliever? Or what agreement has the temple of God with idols?" The obvious answer is *none*. For the sake of the clarity of the gospel we preach, believers must not muddy the doctrinal waters by forging alliances with false religion. Christians need to stop attempting to harmonize the true gospel with satanic lies. Rather than sifting for elements of truth in other religions, the church ought to boldly expose how the false gospel of works is ushering people into hell. In Galatians 5, Paul says that one who compromises the gospel by tolerating those who add works to faith as necessary for salvation are "severed from Christ" and "fallen from grace" (v. 4).

A renewed commitment to *sola fide* would affirm the uniqueness of the biblical gospel and protect the church from the corrupting influence of works-righteousness.

That diminishing commitment to justification by faith alone has likewise inflicted the trend of easy-believism on the church. While Scripture is clear that good works do not contribute to our justification, righteous behavior is nonetheless the essential reality produced by salvation. In his epistle to the Ephesians, Paul declared, "For by grace you have been saved through faith; and that not of yourselves, it is the gift of God; not as a result of works, so that no one may boast. For we are His workmanship, *created in Christ Jesus for good works, which God prepared beforehand so that we would walk in them*" (Eph. 2:8–10, emphasis added). Salvation comes purely by faith, but that transformation immediately demonstrates itself in righteous attitudes and behavior.

The false gospel of easy-believism demands no such proof of the Spirit's transforming work. It effectively treats faith as a work—one that requires no further evidence of repentance or transformation.

In the end, easy-believism amounts to nothing more than *decisional regeneration*, a lie every bit as deadly as works-righteousness. As I explained years ago in *The Gospel According to Jesus*,

> Modern evangelism is preoccupied with decisions, statistics, aisle-walking, gimmicks, prefabricated presentations, pitches, emotional manipulation, and even intimidation. Its message is a cacophony of easy-believism and simplistic appeals. Unbelievers are told that if they invite Jesus into their hearts, accept Him as personal Savior, or believe the facts of the gospel, that is all there is to it. The aftermath is appalling failure, as seen in the lives of millions who have professed faith in Christ with no consequent impact on their behavior. Who knows how many people are deluded into believing they are saved when they are not?[3]

Easy-believism silences the cries of the conscience and encourages false assurance. Countless men and women today expect an eternity in heaven because they once prayed a prayer or made an emotional decision about Christ. Along with others who put their faith in their own pious works, they will one day hear these horrifying words from the Lord: "I never knew you; depart from Me, you who practice lawlessness" (Matt. 7:23).

The book of James says unmistakably, "Faith without works is dead" (James 2:26). James explains that the empty, dead faith of easy-believism is no better than that of demons, who shudder at God's existence but are no less damned (v. 19). According to James, such faith is "useless" (v. 20).

A renewed commitment to *sola fide*, and a biblical understanding of the true faith that justifies—faith in the finished work of Christ alone, faith authenticated through the evidence of a transformed life—would leave no room for the gospel of easy-believism and the false assurance it has sown throughout the church.

SOLA GRATIA

In anticipation of man's capacity to contort faith into the sinner's meritorious work, Scripture makes clear that justification is not only through faith alone, but by divine grace alone. Catholics point to their own rituals as the means of salvation, while other prideful people claim the credit for believing in God and triggering their own salvation. But the doctrine of *sola gratia* destroys all notions of salvation by any cause other than the glorious grace of God. Paul makes that point in Ephesians 2:8–9: "For by grace you have been saved through faith; and *that not of yourselves, it is the gift of God*; not as a result of works, so that no one may boast" (emphasis added).

The biblical doctrine of grace alone corresponds to and is necessitated by man's inability and unwillingness. Sinners have earned and deserve only the wrath of God poured out against their constant and willful rebellion. All stand fully and equally guilty before the Lord: "For all have sinned and fall short of the glory of God" (Rom. 3:23). In Galatians 3:10, Paul writes, "For as many as are of the works of the Law are under a curse; for it is written, 'Cursed is everyone who does not abide by all things written in the book of the Law, to perform them.'" Man's utter corruption prevents him from earning or achieving God's favor in any way. Our salvation "does not depend on the man who wills or the man who runs, but on God who has mercy" (Rom. 9:16). God saves us "not on the basis of deeds which we have done in righteousness, but according to His mercy" (Titus 3:5).

In fact, it's because of our unworthiness that God's saving grace is so amazing. In spite of our wickedness and corruption, He graciously grants us faith, washes us in the blood of His Son, and cloaks us in the flawless righteousness of Christ. Paul writes, "He made Him who knew no sin to be sin on our behalf, so that we might become the righteousness of God in Him" (2 Cor. 5:21). God imputed our wicked lives of sin to Christ, who in His death on the cross had all our sins laid on Him by His Father, so that He paid in full the penalty that was due us. He now imputes the infinitely perfect righteousness of Christ to the account of each believer—all solely as a function of His infinite grace.

But that grace is not a primary feature in the message or the evangelistic strategies that dominate most churches today. Rather than emphasizing the powerful grace of God that alone can overcome man's inability and depravity, modern attractional methods stress the value of cultural relevance and catering to the felt needs of unbelievers. The idea is to tailor the church to appeal to unbelievers, leveraging their tastes and interests to draw them into the fellowship of the church and, eventually, to faith in Christ. That so-called seeker sensitivity is a cynical approach to evangelism that exposes its proponents' lack of confidence in the truth of the Word of God and the power of the Holy Spirit. Ultimately, the strategy is born out of the conviction that it is not God's grace that compels the sinner, but the cleverness of the preacher's sales pitch.

And in the foolish pursuit of fleeting relevance, churches will stop at nothing to attract their target audience. While there are some truly bizarre examples of churches going to extreme lengths to imitate and interest a particular subculture, the majority of churches employing these strategies fall into an increasingly familiar pattern. The worship leaders turn into pop musicians, the preachers transform into comedians and motivational speakers, and worship produced by theological truth is replaced by emotional stimulation that bypasses the mind. Topics like sin, judgment, holiness, godliness, separation from the world, humility, sacrifice, purity, and the need for repentance won't be heard. The goal is to keep it positive, affirming, inoffensive, light, and fun so visitors come back for more.

The conventional wisdom among evangelicals today is that cultural relevance and seeker-sensitive adjustments to the message we proclaim are essential tools for effective evangelism. But the methodology spawned by that philosophy inevitably obscures or totally buries the gospel—the good news of what Christ has done—under a man-centered message that invariably focuses on something the sinner himself must do. It also buries the glory of Christ Jesus, often under a blanket of lights, smoke, and blaring sensual music. Furthermore, from a sheer pragmatic perspective, new-model evangelistic strategies simply don't work. They may sometimes be effective in packing crowds into the church building, but do they truly draw people to Christ? On the contrary, with all their talk about self-esteem, self-worth, self-betterment, and other anthropocentric themes, seeker-sensitive methods tend to shift the sinner's focus inward rather than to the Lord.

True "seekers"—people genuinely seeking God on their own initiative—don't even exist. In Romans 3:11, Paul declares unequivocally, "There is none who seeks for God." Sinners cannot be wooed to the truth by clever marketing and high production value. Christ Himself said, "No one can come to Me unless the Father who sent Me draws him" (John 6:44).

Only through God's gracious gift of faith can anyone be redeemed. God's ability to pursue and draw sinners isn't contingent on the cleverness of the speaker or the talent of the musicians. And it isn't unleashed when the church shamelessly apes the worldly trends of pop culture. Nothing Christians do to adjust or embellish the gospel of Jesus Christ could ever make the message more compelling or the grace of God more potent.

A firm commitment to *sola gratia* would shift the focus of the church away from how it markets itself to the world, and onto the only means of true faith and repentance—the power of the gospel in the work of the Holy Spirit.

SOLI DEO GLORIA

There is no hyperbole in Paul's instructions to the church to glorify the Lord in even life's most mundane activities. He writes,

"Whether, then, you eat or drink or whatever you do, do all to the glory of God" (1 Cor. 10:31). Glorifying God should be our primary goal and our chief motivation. His glory alone ought to be the animating intent behind our every action, thought, and word.

But have you noticed how little you hear about the glory of God lately? Listening to the leading voices in the church, you get the idea that God is more interested in your happiness, fulfillment, and satisfaction than His own glory. The god featured in many sermons today is little more than a genie, eager to fix your problems and make your dreams come true. There's no sense of a higher purpose to life than man's own satisfaction and pleasure, with the Lord depicted as his chief enabler. One of Satan's favorite and most effective strategies is to disguise narcissism with a pious but tawdry façade. Clearly, the deception is working. Many churches are offering not what God seeks, but what is natural to the depraved sinner—his own fulfilled desires. When preachers offer health, wealth, fulfillment, or satisfaction, the sinner is made sovereign. His will must be done, or he won't join!

As a result, rampaging pride and selfishness have infected the church at every level. In the pews, men and women expect God to give them what they desire, fulfilling all their fantasies as He pours out endless blessing and favor, because He loves them so unconditionally and is so happy they finally like Him. Pastors and church leaders compound the problem by living opulent lifestyles that they excuse as proof of God's hearty approval of their ministries. Worse still is the spiritually bankrupt and biblically deficient message from the pulpit that actually incites materialism, covetousness, greed, human pride, earthly affections, and a host of other carnal inclinations set against the glory of God. It should stun such deceivers that God said, "I will not give My glory to another" (Isa. 42:8).

This insidious trend is not isolated to the false prophets of the prosperity gospel. Today, pastors from all denominations and theological persuasions invent an idol who is interested in solving problems and satisfying carnal desires rather than in what the true God is doing by building Christ's church and sanctifying His people. That becomes a significant hindrance to salvation and spiritual growth, and thus hinders the true work of God's kingdom.

The church cannot be a light to the world if it is consumed with narcissistic greed. Christians have nothing to offer unbelievers when they succumb to the same kind of sinful self-interest and self-preoccupation. God's people need to get their eyes off themselves and onto Him. They need to consider the magnitude of His holiness, the fullness of His attributes, and the graciousness of the love He pours out in spite of their repeated failures. They need to echo the words of Paul in Romans 11:36: "For from Him and through Him and to Him are all things. To Him be the glory forever."

God's glory is the dominating reality in the life of every believer. Christians need to get in the habit of asking, "How will this decision, this action, this conversation, along with everything else I do today, bring glory and honor to the Lord?" Submitting everything you do to that test will guard you from the temptation to fixate on your own selfish interests. You won't have time to indulge your selfish desires if you're submitting every aspect of your life to the praise and honor of the Lord.

The glory of God is the overarching purpose behind everything He does. Moreover, it's the purpose behind my life, and the life of every believer. God's people aren't interested in their own achievements. They understand that it is God who accomplishes His will through them, and Him alone who deserves the glory, honor, and praise.

Most lists of the five *solas* conclude with *soli Deo gloria*. That's fitting, because a clear emphasis on God's glory is foundational to all the other pillars of Reformation theology. But I want to end where we began, with our eyes fixed on Christ in His church.

SOLUS CHRISTUS

Salvation is available in Christ alone.

That's not a popular truth these days. In a world where post-modern relativism has run amok, no one wants to hear about the exclusivity of the gospel of Jesus Christ. Even some who call themselves Protestants and evangelicals find that message off-putting and controversial.

Many in the church refuse to let the gospel offend sinners. They think, *You can't tell people they're wrong about the gospel. You can't tell them they're going to hell.* Instead, they want God's Word to be accommodating of error and open to broad and wildly varied interpretations. They want to find room in the plan of redemption to sneak in earnest followers of other faiths. They can't abide the narrow gate, and they go about convincing others that the path to heaven isn't as strict and rigid as it sounds.

Such waffling plays right into the hands of this world's pluralistic philosophy. In this age of tolerance, no one wants to hear that salvation is found only in the person and work of Jesus Christ. Such exclusive claims contradict a world without absolutes, a world dominated by the infantile notion that I should be entitled to determine "my own truth."

But if the church can't hold fast to the truth about Christ—that there is only "one mediator also between God and men, the man Christ Jesus" (1 Tim. 2:5), that "there is salvation in no one else; for there is no other name under heaven that has been given among men by which we must be saved" (Acts 4:12)—then there is no light to bring to this sin-blinded world. Put simply, if you have not explained that faith in Jesus Christ is the *only* way of salvation, you have not preached the gospel.

The church must contend against the intellectual arrogance and religious pluralism of this rebellious world by faithfully upholding this most unpopular of all biblical truths about the Lord—namely, that He is as He stated: "the way, and the truth, and the life; no one comes to the Father but through Me" (John 14:6).

Moreover, the church must be devoted to Christ. The "proof of your faith," Peter said, is that "though you have not seen Him, you love Him, and though you do not see Him now, but believe in Him, you greatly rejoice with joy inexpressible and full of glory" (1 Peter 1:7–8). God's people must not forsake their first love. As we saw in the Lord's letters to the churches, that's how the precipitous and deadly slide to Laodicea begins. Put simply, there is no greater defense against spiritual lethargy, compromise, corruption, and apostasy than faithfully stoking the flames of your love for Christ.

That's why preaching Christ isn't a preference; it's a necessity. Pastors who don't preach Christ are failing the goats and starving the sheep. Of the almost fifty years I have taught in the pulpit at Grace Community Church, roughly twenty-five of them were spent preaching through the Gospels. When you add all we've learned about Jesus in our study of the Epistles and in the Old Testament, I dare say not a Sunday goes by that we're not gazing into the character and nature of our glorious Lord. It's crucial for God's people to know the full revelation about Christ if they're going to truly love Him. And that love is vital to the life of the church and its usefulness to the work of God's kingdom.

With all that in mind, some time ago I wrote a short statement about the rich depths of loving Christ as He is revealed in Scripture. It warms my love to revisit it from time to time, and I trust it will rekindle your love for Him, too:

> We love Christ. We love Christ who is the eternal Son, one in nature with the eternal Father and the eternal Spirit; the triune God. We love Christ who is the Creator and life-giver, as well as the sustainer of the universe and all who live in it. We love Christ who is the virgin-born Son of God and Son of Man, fully divine and fully human.

We love Christ who is the one whose life on earth perfectly pleased God, and whose righteousness is given to all who by grace through faith become one with Him. We love Christ who is the only acceptable sacrifice for sin that pleases God, and whose death under divine judgment, paid in full the penalty for the sins of His people, providing for them forgiveness and eternal life. We love Christ who is alive, having been raised from the dead by the Father, validating His work of atonement, and providing resurrection for the sanctification and glorification of the elect to bring them safely into His heavenly presence.

We love Christ who is at the Father's throne interceding for all believers. We love Christ who is God's chosen Prophet, Priest, and King, proclaiming truth, mediating for His church, and reigning over His kingdom forever. We love Christ who will certainly and suddenly return from heaven to rapture His church, unleash judgment on the wicked, bring promised salvation to the Jews and the nations, and establish His millennial reign on earth. We love Christ who will, after that earthly reign, destroy the universe, finally judge all sinners and send them to hell, then create the new heavens and the new earth where He will dwell forever with His saints in glory, joy, and love. This is the Christ we love; this is the Christ we preach. And we love Him because He first loved us.

If there is any hope for a new reformation and revival today, it is that the church will submit to the authority and sufficiency of Scripture, that it will faithfully proclaim the message of justification by grace alone through faith alone, that God's people will devote themselves to glorifying Him in all things, and that they hold fast to the gospel of Jesus Christ in loving devotion to their Savior.

Acknowledgments

S pecial thanks to the editorial staff at Grace to You—with particular gratitude to Jeremiah Johnson, who skillfully oversaw the assembly and editorial process on this manuscript from its inception as raw sermon transcripts to its final polished and pithy form.

Notes

Chapter 1: Calling the Church to Repent

1. Matthew Meade, "Remedying the Sin of Ejecting God's Ministers," in C. Matthew McMahon, ed., *Discovering the Wickedness of our Heart* (Crossville, TN: Puritan Publications, 2016), 174.

2. Iain Murray, ed., *Sermons of the Great Ejection* (London: Banner of Truth Trust, 1962), 8.

3. John Buxton Marsden, *The History of the Later Puritans: From the Opening of the Civil War in 1642, to the Ejection of the Non-Conforming Clergy in 1662* (London: Hamilton, Adams, & Co., 1854), 469–70.

4. Ibid., 480.

5. J. C. Ryle, "Baxter and His Times," in *Lectures Delivered Before the Young Men's Christian Association*, vol. 8 (London: James Nisbet and Co., 1853), 379.

6. The Catholic Church still offers indulgences to this day, although it is no longer the monumental fundraising boon it once was. Instead, Catholics can receive indulgences for simple "acts of piety and devotion," like following the Pope on Twitter.

7. Helmut T. Lehmann, ed., Theodore G. Tappert, ed. and trans., *Luther's Works (vol. 54): Table Talk* (Philadelphia: Fortress, 1967), 193–94.

8. Martin Brecht in Helmut T. Lehmann, ed., James L. Schaaf trans., *Luther's Works (vol. 1): Martin Luther* (Philadelphia: Fortress, 1985), 460.

9. Pew Research Center, "U.S. Protestants Are Not Defined by Reformation-Era Controversies 500 Years Later" (August 31, 2017), http://www.pewforum.org/2017/08/31/u-s-protestants-are-not-defined-by-reformation-era-controversies-500-years-later/.

10. Kevin Porter, "Andy Stanley at Catalyst Cincinnati: Don't Put Theology Above Ministry, Let Cultural Issues Bump People Out," *The Christian Post* (April 23, 2016), https://www.christianpost.com/news/andy-stanley-at-catalyst-cincinnati-dont-put-theology-above-ministry-let-cultural-issues-bump-people-out-162414/.

11. Tertullian, *On Prescription Against Heretics* in Alexander Roberts and James Donaldson, trans., *Ante-Nicene Fathers*, 10 vols. (New York: Christian Literature Publishing Co., 1885) 3:260.

12. John Granger Cook, *Roman Attitudes Toward the Christians: From Claudius to Hadrian* (Tübingen: Mohr Siebeck, 2010), 77–78. Cf. Tacitus, *Annals*, 15:44.

Chapter 3: The Loveless Church—Ephesus

1. Robin Waterfield, ed., *The First Philosophers: The Presocratics and Sophists* (Oxford: Oxford University, 2000), 45.

2. Quoted in Merrill C. Tenney, *Interpreting Revelation* (Grand Rapids: Eerdmans, 1957), 61.

3. Clement, *The Stromata, or Miscellanies*, in Alexander Roberts and James Donaldson eds., *The Ante-Nicene Fathers*, 9 vols. (Edinburgh: T&T Clark, 1873) 2:373.

Chapter 4: The Persecuted Church—Smyrna

1. Quoted in Alexander Roberts, Sir James Donaldson, eds., *The Ante-Nicene Fathers*, 10 vols. (New York: Scribners, 1905), 1:41.

2. Ibid.

3. Ibid., 42.

Chapter 5: The Compromising Church—Pergamum

1. William M. Ramsey, *The Letters to the Seven Churches of Asia* (London: Hodder & Stoughton, 1906), 281.

2. Edwin Yamauchi, *New Testament Cities in Western Asia Minor* (Grand Rapids: Baker, 1980), 35–36.

3. "U2charist," *Wikipedia*, https://en.wikipedia.org/wiki/U2charist.

4. Life.Church, "At the Movies," *Life.Church*, https://www.life.church/watch/at-the-movies/.

5. Katherine Weber, "Perry Noble No Regret Over Playing AC/DC 'Highway to Hell' for Easter Service: 'I'd Do It Again - But Better!,'" *The Christian Post*, March 25, 2016, https://www.christianpost.com/news/perry-noble-megachurch-ac-dc-highway-to-hell-easter-160107/.

Chapter 7: The Dead Church—Sardis

1. Robert L. Thomas, *Revelation 1–7: An Exegetical Commentary* (Chicago: Moody, 1992), 241.

Chapter 8: The Faithful Church—Philadelphia

1. William M. Ramsey, *The Letters to the Seven Churches of Asia* (London: Hodder & Stoughton, 1906), 397.

Chapter 9: The Lukewarm Church—Laodicea

1. John R. W. Stott, *What Christ Thinks of the Church* (Grand Rapids: Eerdmans, 1980), 116.

2. Alfred John Church and William Jackson Brodribb, trans., *Annals of Tacitus*, xiv:27 (New York: Macmillan, 1895), 268.

3. J. B. Lightfoot, *Saint Paul's Epistles to the Colossians and to Philemon* (London: Macmillan, 1879), 20–21.

4. D. Martyn Lloyd-Jones, *Studies in the Sermon on the Mount* (Grand Rapids: Eerdmans, 1974), 2:248.

Chapter 10: The Need for a New Reformation

1. Sarah Young, *Jesus Calling* (Nashville: Thomas Nelson, 2004), xiii.

2. John MacArthur, *Our Sufficiency in Christ* (Dallas: Word Publishing, 1991), 58.

3. John MacArthur, *The Gospel According to Jesus*, rev. ed. (Grand Rapids: Zondervan, 2008), 91.

Steps to Peace With God

1. God's Purpose: Peace and Life

God loves you and wants you to experience peace and life—
abundant and eternal.

The Bible says ...

"We have peace with God through our Lord
Jesus Christ." *Romans 5:1, NKJV*

"For God so loved the world that He gave His
only begotten Son, that whoever believes in
Him should not perish but have everlasting life."
John 3:16, NKJV

"I have come that they may have life, and that
they may have it more abundantly."
John 10:10, NKJV

Since God planned for
us to have peace and the
abundant life right now,
why are most people not
having this experience?

2. Our Problem: Separation From God

God created us in His own image to have an abundant life. He did
not make us as robots to automatically love and obey Him, but
gave us a will and a freedom of choice.

We chose to disobey God and go our own willful way. We still
make this choice today. This results in separation from God.

The Bible says ...

"For all have sinned and fall
short of the glory of God."
Romans 3:23, NKJV

"For the wages of sin is death, but
the gift of God is eternal life in
Christ Jesus our Lord."
Romans 6:23, NKJV

Our choice results
in separation from God.

Our Attempts

Through the ages, individuals have tried in many ways to bridge this gap ... without success ...

The Bible says ...

"There is a way that seems right to a man, but its end is the way of death."
Proverbs 14:12, NKJV

"But your iniquities have separated you from your God; and your sins have hidden His face from you, so that He will not hear."
Isaiah 59:2, NKJV

There is only one remedy for this problem of separation.

3. God's Remedy: The Cross

Jesus Christ is the only answer to this problem. He died on the cross and rose from the grave, paying the penalty for our sin and bridging the gap between God and people.

The Bible says ...

"For there is one God and one Mediator between God and men, the Man Christ Jesus."
1 Timothy 2:5, NKJV

"For Christ also suffered once for sins, the just for the unjust, that He might bring us to God."
1 Peter 3:18, NKJV

"But God shows his love for us in that while we were still sinners, Christ died for us." *Romans 5:8, ESV*

God has provided the only way ... we must make the choice ...

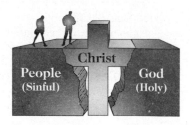

4. Our Response: Receive Christ

We must trust Jesus Christ and receive Him by personal invitation.

The Bible says ...

"Behold, I stand at the door and knock. If anyone hears My voice and opens the door, I will come in to him and dine with him, and he with Me." *Revelation 3:20, NKJV*

"But to all who did receive him, who believed in his name, he gave the right to become children of God." *John 1:12, ESV*

"If you confess with your mouth that Jesus is Lord and believe in your heart that God raised him from the dead, you will be saved." *Romans 10:9, ESV*

Are you here ... or here?

Is there any good reason why you cannot receive Jesus Christ right now?

How to Receive Christ:

1. Admit your need (say, "I am a sinner").
2. Be willing to turn from your sins (repent) and ask for God's forgiveness.
3. Believe that Jesus Christ died for you on the cross and rose from the grave.
4. Through prayer, invite Jesus Christ to come in and control your life through the Holy Spirit (receive Jesus as Lord and Savior).

What to Pray:

Dear God,

I know that I am a sinner. I want to turn from my sins, and I ask for Your forgiveness. I believe that Jesus Christ is Your Son. I believe He died for my sins and that You raised Him to life. I want Him to come into my heart and to take control of my life. I want to trust Jesus as my Savior and follow Him as my Lord from this day forward.

In Jesus' Name, amen.

_____   _____
Date   Signature

God's Assurance: His Word

If you prayed this prayer,

the Bible says ...

"For 'everyone who calls on the name of the Lord will be saved.'"
Romans 10:13, ESV

Did you sincerely ask Jesus Christ to come into your life?
Where is He right now? What has He given you?

"For by grace you have been saved through faith. And this is not your
own doing; it is the gift of God, not a result of works, so that no one may
boast." *Ephesians 2:8–9, ESV*

the Bible says ...

"He who has the Son has life; he who does not have the Son of God does
not have life. These things I have written to you who believe in the name of
the Son of God, that you may know that you have eternal life, and that you
may continue to believe in the name of the Son of God."
1 John 5:12–13, NKJV

Receiving Christ, we are born into God's family through the
supernatural work of the Holy Spirit, who indwells every believer.
This is called regeneration or the "new birth."

This is just the beginning of a wonderful new life in Christ. To deepen
this relationship you should:

1. Read your Bible every day to know Christ better.
2. Talk to God in prayer every day.
3. Tell others about Christ.
4. Worship, fellowship, and serve with other Christians in a church where
   Christ is preached.
5. As Christ's representative in a needy world, demonstrate your new life by
   your love and concern for others.

God bless you as you do.

Franklin Graham

If you want further help in the decision you have made, write to:
Billy Graham Evangelistic Association
1 Billy Graham Parkway, Charlotte, NC 28201-0001

1-877-2GRAHAM (1-877-247-2426)
BillyGraham.org/commitment